EVP
Electronic Voice Phenomenon

Massachusetts Ghostly Voices

Michael Markowicz

4880 Lower Valley Road, Atglen, Pennsylvania 19310

Materials recorded on the CD are copyrighted by the author.

Photographs, unless otherwise noted, are courtesy of the author.

Radio Shack and Sony are registered trademarks. Please note that product endorsements are solely author choice and this text is not meant to relay specific buying patterns.

Please follow all trespassing and related laws when attempting to secure EVPs.

Schiffer Books are available at special discounts for bulk purchases for sales promotions or premiums. Special editions, including personalized covers, corporate imprints, and excerpts can be created in large quantities for special needs. For more information contact the publisher:

Schiffer Publishing Ltd.
4880 Lower Valley Road
Atglen, PA 19310
Phone: (610) 593-1777; Fax: (610) 593-2002
E-mail: Info@schifferbooks.com

For the largest selection of fine reference books on this and related subjects, please visit our web site at:

www.schifferbooks.com

We are always looking for people to write books on new and related subjects. If you have an idea for a book please contact us at the above address.

This book may be purchased from the publisher. Include $5.00 for shipping. Please try your bookstore first. You may write for a free catalog.

In Europe, Schiffer books are distributed by
Bushwood Books
6 Marksbury Ave.
Kew Gardens
Surrey TW9 4JF England
Phone: 44 (0) 20 8392-8585; Fax: 44 (0) 20 8392-9876
E-mail: info@bushwoodbooks.co.uk
Website: www.bushwoodbooks.co.uk

Copyright © 2009 by Michael Markowicz
Library of Congress Control Number: 2009927048

All rights reserved. No part of this work may be reproduced or used in any form or by any means—graphic, electronic, or mechanical, including photocopying or information storage and retrieval systems—without written permission from the publisher.
The scanning, uploading and distribution of this book or any part thereof via the Internet or via any other means without the permission of the publisher is illegal and punishable by law. Please purchase only authorized editions and do not participate in or encourage the electronic piracy of copyrighted materials.
"Schiffer," "Schiffer Publishing Ltd. & Design," and the "Design of pen and ink well" are registered trademarks of Schiffer Publishing Ltd.

Designed by Stephanie Daugherty
Type set in Krystoid/CityDLig/ Zurich BT/OCR A Extended

ISBN: 978-0-7643-3359-0
Printed in China

Dedication

For my mother, who came to me, in spirit, when I got my first digital recorder, allowing me to understand that the electronic voice phenomenon is real.

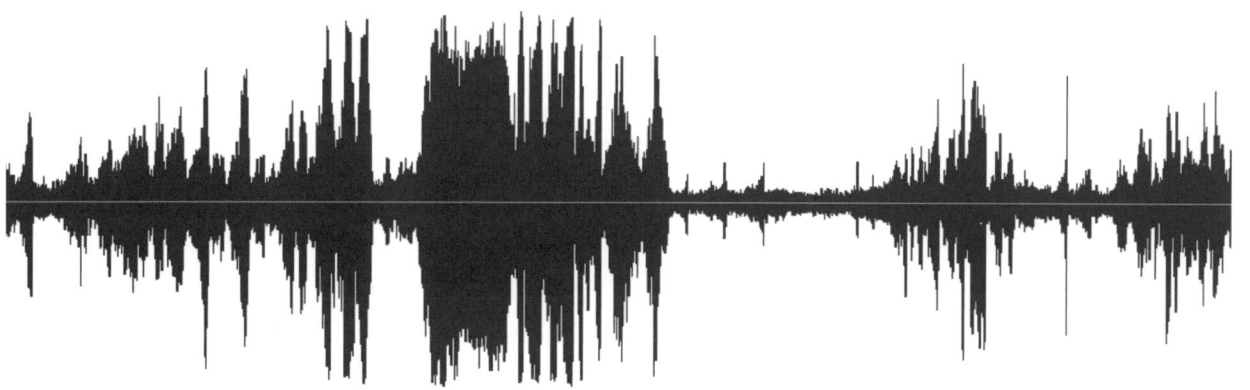

Acknowledgments

When doors open, walk through and take on the experience to make it your own. I would like to thank everyone who I have recorded for over the years, for if it were not for you allowing me into your homes and businesses, I would not have written this book.

For my wife, Paula, who has put up with me hauling equipment in and out of the house, and being patient, as thousands of hours passed by, watching me work with my headphones on. Thank you to my daughter, Deliah, for showing me, in your honesty, at the age of three, that spirits do communicate with us.

Thank you to all of the B.O.O.O. members, Jordie, Sally, Patrick, Marc, and Kristin, whom I cut my teeth with in the field of paranormal investigating. *(I miss the duck.)* Thank you to Russ Hannigan, for teaching me the ins and outs of program production from East Bridgewater's cable station. To Anne Kerrigan, for producing *East Bridgewater's Most Haunted*, and for all of the hours spent behind the Apple. She has become a valuable partner on the road to all things paranormal. Thank you to Mike Dieser, for his friendship and partnership in Spiritcom research. He truly has opened my eyes to what is possible in the field of paranormal studies. Thank you to the *Spooky South Coast* Radio crew, Tim Weisberg, Matt Costa and Matt Moniz for airing my work, and, as always, thank you for your help with the investigations. Thanks to Ron Kolek and Maureen Wood, from *Ghost Chronicles* radio show. If it wasn't for Ron I never would have started my presentations.

Special thanks goes to Robyne Marie from *Lights Out* radio for all of the opportunities, and those still yet to come, but more importantly, for believing in my work. Thanks to Elizabeth Russell, at the Bay State Paranormal Center, for giving me a place to teach, present data and for the investigation opportunities. Thank you to Chris Balzano, for including me in his books and for all of the kind words.

Playing Your CD

In order to hear the audio clips, place the CD in a computer drive and click on the folder on the monitor to open it. There you will find 90 tracks of various sounds, to play along as you read through the chapters. They are numbered accordingly. For an appropriate experience, it is best to read the background that accompanies each track. The duration of these clips is short. It is best to use a player that has a pause button that is easily accessible for replay.

Contents

Author's Note 8

Introduction: How I See It 9

1: Different Devices 16

    Track 01 (Time Length 01:11)   Track 07 (00:23)
    Track 02 (00:03)   Track 08 (00:01)
    Track 03 (00:09)   Track 09 (00:02)
    Track 04 (00:04)   Track 10 (00:01)
    Track 05 (00:04)   Track 11 (00:01)
    Track 06 (00:06)   Track 12 (00:02)

2: My Beginning: This Old House 32

    Track 13 (00:19)   Track 16 (00:02)
    Track 14 (00:04)   Track 17 (00:01)
    Track 15 (00:01)   Track 18 (00:02)

3: The Old Duxbury House, Duxbury 37

    Track 19 (00:02)   Track 24 (00:02)
    Track 20 (00:04)   Track 25 (00:02)
    Track 21 (00:01)   Track 26 (00:13)
    Track 22 (00:01)   Track 27 (00:05)
    Track 23 (00:02)

4: The First Church, Weymouth 43

    Track 28 (00:15)   Track 29 (00:05)

5: The North Church, Hingham 47

    Track 30 (00:02)   Track 31 (00:02)

Contents

6: Cordage Park, Plymouth 51

    TRACK 32 (00:02)   TRACK 34 (00:02)
    TRACK 33 (00:05)   TRACK 35 (00:02)

7: Fort Revere, Hull 56

    TRACK 36 (00:02)   TRACK 38 (00:01)
    TRACK 37 (00:04)   TRACK 39 (00:01)

8: Palmer River, Rehoboth 60

    Track 40 (00:04)

9: Guthrie Residence, East Bridgewater 64

    TRACK 41 (00:01)   TRACK 48 (00:02)
    TRACK 42 (00:01)   TRACK 49 (00:02)
    TRACK 43 (00:02)   TRACK 50 (00:04)
    TRACK 44 (00:01)   TRACK 51 (00:04)
    TRACK 45 (00:01)   TRACK 52 (00:03)
    TRACK 46 (00:01)   TRACK 53 (00:11)
    TRACK 47 (00:01)

10: A Private Business, Brockton 70

    TRACK 54 (00:11)   TRACK 58 (00:04)
    TRACK 55 (00:05)   TRACK 59 (00:04)
    TRACK 56 (00:05)   TRACK 60 (00:04)
    TRACK 57 (00:04)

11: William L. White Mansion, Taunton 76

    TRACK 61 (00:05)   TRACK 63 (00:05)
    TRACK 62 (00:04)

12: McArdell Residence, Plymouth 81

    TRACK 64 (00:10)   TRACK 65 (00:04)

Contents   7

13: The Town Hall, East Bridgewater — 87

TRACK 66 (00:05)   TRACK 67 (00:10)

14: The Inn on Washington Square, Salem — 92

TRACK 68 (00:12)   TRACK 72 (00:16)
TRACK 69 (00:03)   TRACK 73 (00:12)
TRACK 70 (00:06)   TRACK 74 (00:03)
TRACK 71 (00:03)

15: The Fearing Tavern, Wareham — 100

TRACK 75 (00:05)   TRACK 78 (00:03)
TRACK 76 (00:09)   TRACK 79 (00:25)
TRACK 77 (00:01)

16: First Parrish Church, Norwell — 108

TRACK 80 (00:43)   TRACK 84 (00:06)
TRACK 81 (00:16)   TRACK 85 (00:17)
TRACK 82 (00:06)   TRACK 86 (00:26)
TRACK 83 (00:13)   TRACK 87 (00:13)

17: The Great Singularity and the Oneness — 118

TRACK 88 (00:03)   TRACK 89 (00:03)

18: Becoming Clairaudient — 122

Conclusions — 126

Track 90 (00:21)

Resources — 128

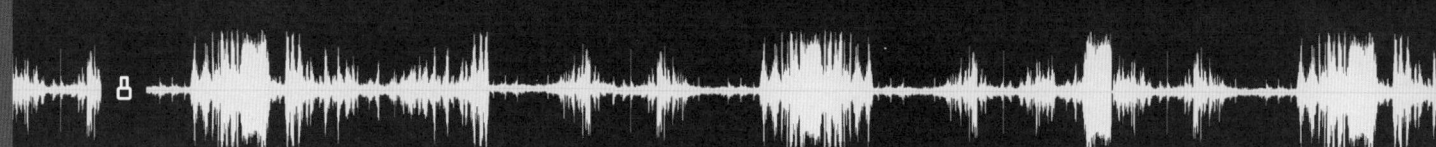

Author's Note

[Play track 01]

Hello, thank you for purchasing *EVP: Electronic Voice Phenomenon; Massachusetts Ghostly Voices*. I am the Author, Michael Markowicz. The electronic voice phenomenon has been around for as long as people have been recording sound. Nobody really knows why these voices continue to show up on audio recordings. I chose to study this fascinating subject as it is an area of paranormal study that anyone may obtain excellent results from.

I have discovered, possibly, two separate dimensions where communication has occurred. Ninety-nine percent of all the recordings that I have to date come from a place that I call the Great Singularity. The other, only two recordings, are in a place I call the Oneness. Both are psychological in nature. I am of no one particular faith or religion and I do believe in God. However, I think that combining technology and spirituality, will give better results.

There are many technical people who choose to reveal the mystery of the electronic voice phenomenon purely in a scientific manner, and wish not to delve into spiritual matters at all. To me, that is like studying the engine of a race car and neglecting the driver, but still expecting to win the race.

Thank you again for purchasing the book.

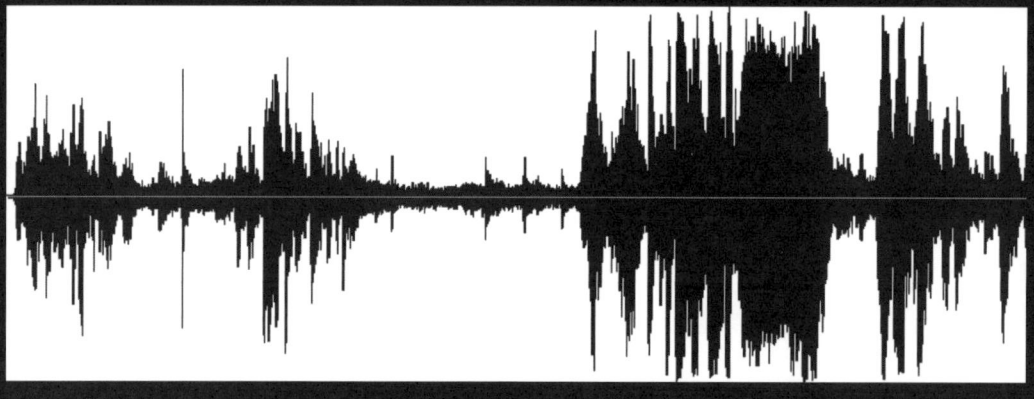

Introduction
How I See It

Welcome to the world of the electronic voice phenomenon or "EVP" as it is widely referred to. Wikipedia states:

"Electronic Voice Phenomena (EVP) are sections of static noise on the radio or electronic recording that some listeners believe sound like voices speaking words. Paranormal investigators sometimes interpret these noises as the voices of ghosts or spirits. Recording EVP has become a technique for those who attempt to contact the souls of dead loved ones or during ghost hunting activities. According to Parapsychologist Konstantin Raudive, who popularized the idea, EVP are typically brief – usually, a link of a word or short phrase. Skeptics of the paranormal attribute the voice-like aspect of the sounds to apophenia (finding of significance or connections between insignificant or unrelated phenomena), auditory pareidolia (interpreting random sounds into voices in their own language which might otherwise sound like random noise to a foreign speaker), artifacts due to low quality equipment and simple hoaxes. Likewise, some reported EVP can be attributed to radio interference or other well documented phenomena."

Basically, an EVP is noted when voices appear on recorded media that were not present during the original recording session. Or were they? There are several schools of thought on just where these voices emanate. The most popular theory is that the voices come from disembodied people from beyond the grave. This has been proven by people who have recorded loved ones, only to realize they have captured their voices some time later. I say it is "proven" because they believe the voice to actually be the person who has recently deceased.

Another belief is that the voices are coming from us and they interact with the "Great Singularity" (or purgatory) and our world in a complete psychological, conscious, and sub-conscious world as a whole, which I will cover later.

Still, there are some who believe that these voices are nothing more than radio cross-talk, which is the sound that seems to bleed over from a radio station's powerful transmission and, in turn, saturates the existing recordings with interference (similar to catching someone else's conversation on a phone line). I also have an example of this, which will be noted in a later chapter.

Sound is an amazing thing, when you stop and consider the ways we receive it. According to Psychoacoustics, "Not only is it perceived as a mechanical wave, but mediums and psychics hear voices and sounds in their brain, as though they had been planted. Hearing is not a purely mechanical phenomenon of wave propagation, but is also a sensory and perceptual event. When a person hears something, that something arrives at the ear as a mechanical sound wave traveling through the air but within the ear and it is transformed into neural action potentials. These nerve pulses then travel to the brain where they are perceived. Hence, in many problems in acoustics, such as for audio processing, it is advantageous to take into account not just the mechanics of the environment, but also the fact that both the ear and the brain are involved in a person's listening experience." The human element of sound perception adds to the spiritual aspect of what is going on around us.

How can anyone with an open mind listen to these voices and not be fascinated by what they are hearing? The mere existence of this phenomena itself lends us a glimpse of God's work at hand. Yes, God. It is my belief that the world was purposefully created, in addition to the Universe as a whole. That is, if you take life-after-death as being possible and that God does exist. I do. Based on the apparent evidence, it tells me that there is much more going on than what we can perceive. Only now, science, by the way of physics, is telling us that there may be something to what people have known for quite sometime about the paranormal world. That it absolutely exists! At least science is considering it now, with the advent of the String Theory and Multi Dimension/Multi Universe Theory. For the first time in history, science and the paranormal community are finding common ground. What an odd occurrence!

So, what do these recordings represent then? Are they just radio waves caught up in the electronic workings of the recorder? Are they really the voices from the dead? After studying these recordings for sometime, I believe there are several things going on here. One, is that I do believe that these are the voices of people who have transitioned over into the unknown. They speak to each other in normal conversations just like we would today. They speak to us, as just about anyone who has ever recorded these voices for themselves may very well know. They sometimes even answer our questions, however, whether the answer is true or not is still yet to be determined.

There are voices that I have recorded that are wispy and light, much like a summer breeze through a screen door, which make up most of the recordings that I have, to date, and number in the thousands. I have also found that there is a mix of light, airy voices, as well as stronger, more definite ones, which may be the result of an accumulation of energy. The more energy that is gathered, perhaps, the louder that voice can be heard. Then, there are those voices that are like a storm of energy – loud and clear. These are the most fascinating recordings of all, although the message, in and of itself, may not seem to be, at the time. The ease of understanding the message is very moving, upon hearing it for the first time. Why the differences in volume and clarity? Aren't they all coming from the same place? Are there volumes to people's souls like the difference in wattage in light bulbs? Can it be that the better a person you are, the brighter your soul shines, and, so, the louder your voice can be heard and recorded? What about the EVP from a male who tells me, "I hate the children."? Surely, he is not one of strong light. Or is he? Maybe it depends on how you use

that light? This appears to me to be true. I believe there is a mix of good and bad people together, existing in a common enough place that they are all able to be recorded. This is surely by design.

There are even voices that seem to be from the past. I remember stories from researchers who have taken their recording equipment to the fields of Gettysburg and captured the soldiers marching, bugles bellowing out commands, along with the sounds of drumming. Surely, these are not current events, as there were no re-enactments going on at the time. It seems that these soldiers are still on the battle field, fighting for what they believed in, at that time. Even if it was over 130 years ago, everything that was going on, continues to occur even today.

This is an interesting example of what may be happening. Perhaps they have not fully crossed over, and they are in between earth and heaven, in a place that was designed for all of those who are not moving on into the light. This is a popular theory; however, in my opinion, it appears that it could be valid. I understand that the church doesn't adhere to the "purgatory" idea any longer, but it makes sense when trying to understand just where these voices might be coming from. Our minds and hearts will determine what kind of life we may lead when we pass on. After all, at that point, we no longer have a physical body. At least this is how I see it to be. Isn't this the basis of what we call a haunting? Some spirit, who stays at their home, or place of work, or maybe even an extremely important position in their life, that keeps playing it over and over? If you are not ready to go "into the light," as a lot of people believe happens, then where do you go? What a comforting notion to think that we may be able to hold onto our human nature by staying close to it in some dimension that has been set up for us to continue to live in. It must be a different dimension, but similar, which must be why we can record the EVP. The other world is right on top of us!

They are so close, in fact, that we can take pictures of them, video tape them moving about and even record their voices. We can be physically touched by them, as I have been, several times. We can also walk right through them and feel the chill. We smell the cigar and cigarette smoke because they were smokers, and still smoke. Even perfume can linger in the air, if they choose. They will speak to us in our ear and, again, this has happened to me, as well. They have the ability to interact with us in our daily lives and influence us as they go.

All of this is by design or it would not be. Like gravity, it has to have been built or it would not exist, in the first place. We live in a physical world, but we are not limited by it. Energy moves in and out of our plane of existence naturally, which is how these spirits go about their business, naturally. Well that's good for us because it means our loved ones are close by at all times, if they haven't moved on into the light that is. But why didn't they, if they were good people? Why didn't they go to heaven? There must be a reason for it.

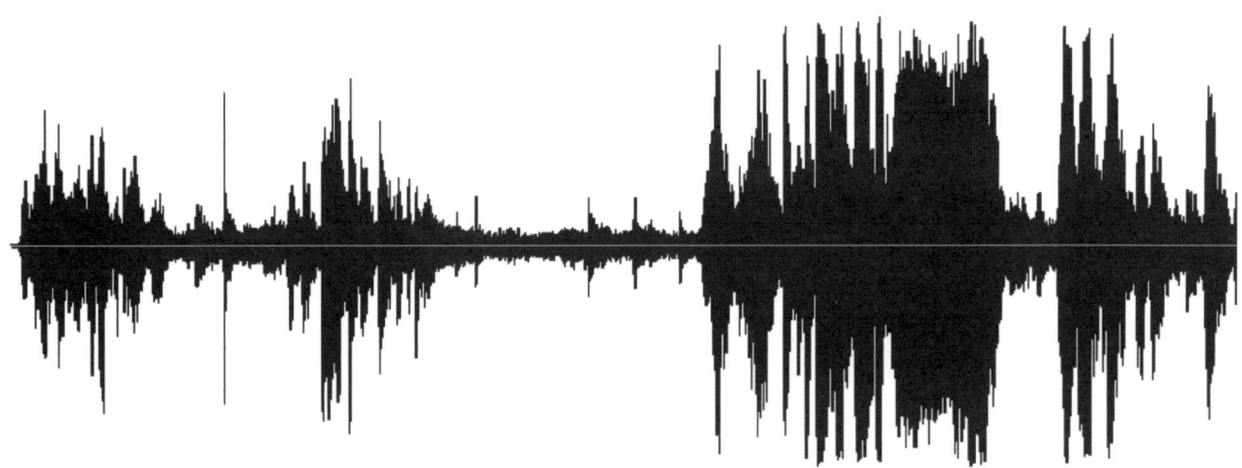

Why Not Heaven?

I need to delve deeper into the whereabouts of these people who are interacting with us and where they are going. We have Heaven and Earth and the space in between. This space I call the Great Singularity which is also known as purgatory. Often described as a waiting place for the time when heaven will open its doors, or the pearly gates, to allow all the lost souls to enter God's kingdom. I call it the Great Singularity because it seems to suit most of the psychological aspects of the people I have been recording as EVPs.

I say psychological, because you do not take a physical body with you when you transition into the next phase of life. You have your mind, although there are talks of an ethereal body that is obtained and can only be one of comfort as a reminder of one's former self. Self is what I believe makes up the Great Singularity, at least in the aspects of thought processes. It is made up of people who still think like a human being on Earth and not one who has learned *not* to think like one. Ego, possessiveness, guilt, and the like are things that can't be taken with you into the next level of life or Heaven. The recordings I have collected reveal people who appear to be living much as they did here on the Earth Plane and are still holding onto that very life even though it is gone. Everyone will move from a world of little spirituality and much physicality to a world of much spirituality and little actual physical contact. You still can't take it with you.

The Bible has alluded to other dimensions or thrones. "For by Him were all things created, that are in Heaven, and that are in Earth, visible and invisible, whether they be thrones or dominions, or principalities or powers: all things were created by Him and for Him." Is this passage a clue to the levels of existence that await us all?

There is also a sing-song quality about the way EVPs sometimes sound. Why are they singing simple sentences and not just saying them as any normal person would? Time and time again I have recorded the sing-song fashion of speaking or cadence. But why is it so important to sing? I have recordings of men, women and children speaking in this way. Music must have an important relevance in some way as to cause so many people to be singing.

I have a theory as to why this is, and I liken it to a child in the stands of a NASCAR race. He is holding a car with his favorite driver's number on it. The child makes the sounds of the cars just as they pass by him as they race around the track. So the child mimics that in which he wants so badly, to be a race car driver. *ZOOOM* as he moves the car through the air. What if we are able to see something from the Great Singularity that we too want but cannot have? What would we say in a mimicking fashion to show something of such great importance? Just as we are able to be aware of the spirit world, so too does the spirit world, as in the Great Singularity, know of a more spiritual world as well. What and where is *that* place then? Psalm 100:2 in the Bible says "Serve the Lord with gladness: come before His presence with singing."

Music is one of the liberal arts and sciences for us, as a fundamental of learning. Music for the Great Singularity is important because it represents something very important to them, as seen and felt by them. From there on, the closer to God you get, the more of yourself you must give and accept the same from others. Giving and receiving is the soul of life. To sing is the gift you give from the Great Singularity and that's probably all you can give, the song of love that comes from within, given to everyone who will hear it. To move on from there you must prepare to shed your mortal coil of "human" thought processes and egotistical aspects before moving onto the true gift of song, worthy of praising God in His presence. This place I will call the Oneness or Heaven, as it contains every soul ever created, that is worthy to stand in the presence of Him. That would certainly account for the sing-song fashion of speaking these EVPs have acquired, wouldn't it? Why else is it so important to sing from the spiritual world? Because they can hear and feel it like the heat from the Sun and everyone there is trying to move out from the shadows (of themselves) and into the light where singing is the result from sharing your soul in a fantastic rhythmic "OM," given up to God. The gift is our ability to share in this choir of knowledge, feeling it and understanding it.

To get back to the recordings in general, I only have the voices of people in different stages of life. No angels giving me vast knowledge of Heaven or demons telling me of pending doom. That's not to say that neither of them exist, just that I don't have any recordings of them. I do believe that if you are a decent person, then you undoubtedly will be the same person on the other side. If you are a bad, nasty person in this life, so too will you be in the next. Tormenting and taking from people in the next life may lead to a bad haunting from our standpoint. The greedy lustful souls of days gone by may return for a taste of the lives they had known and wish to live once again. Possession is a rare but real condition and I have not had any experiences relating to the topic, thankfully. But I have heard of spirits following you home from a recording session from a haunted home or other location only to start becoming a nuisance in your life. So be careful to thank the spirits before and after entering a haunted house. You just never know.

And this is why I take the standpoint of truly believing in God and His work. I'd rather be right in this belief than not believing at all and leaving it all up to a scientific standpoint alone only to be proven wrong later when I need it most. Would *you* take that chance?

And so we have Earth, the Great Singularity and the Oneness. Three different dimensions of life have been recorded from using the same digital recorder. I believe these recordings represent a view of God's work, unlike any other in the sense of physical evidence. There is a world interlacing with ours and we are only now able to capture a glimpse of what it must be like to be there by examining the evidence we obtain from it.

Of course, this is all speculation, however, I have moved from hypothesis to theory with the evidence contained herein. This book contains real accounts of paranormal activity as told to me by the people who have experienced it for themselves. The CD that accompanies this book has the actual EVPs that were recorded from their homes and businesses and are ready to be played as you read along.

When you see,

[Play track xx]

in the text, simply click on the corresponding file on your computer screen to play the track. Adjust the volume so it is at a comfortable listening level. A good quality set of headphones will reveal finer detail in these recordings and often make it easier to hear the EVP. A good set of speakers will also help in revealing the voices if you are using outside speakers and not headphones.

You may have to repeat playing the track several times in order to hear the voice pop out at you. It takes practice sometimes to hear the voices. It is surprising when it happens!

Remember, read the subject surrounding the EVP so you have a better understanding of what I believe has been said on the recording. This information may change according to the listener. For example, I may hear "the wet dog" and you may hear "the white dog" which is entirely different.

I have played recordings for people only to find that they do not hear what I do. Instead, they are hearing a passage with more syllables and a longer sentence but with the same content or meaning. This is one of the strange abilities that EVPs place upon people; perceptions change from person to person and so, too, may the sound of the EVP.

Regardless, I invite you to enjoy this journey into EVP phenomena.

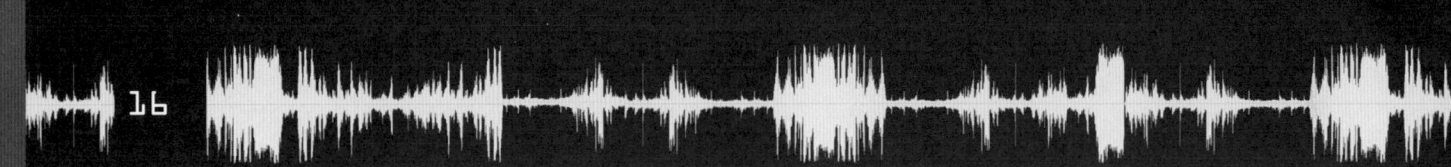

1

Different Devices

It is believed that EVPs must obey God's laws of physics or they cannot be recorded. What if, though, they are obeying God's laws but we are not able to detect it yet. Sir Isaac Newton discovered gravity, but up until then, no one new gravity existed. Life was just *as is*. So maybe we will discover just what mechanism these EVPs use in order to communicate someday, but for now, all methods work in capturing the voices.

Everything that I have used to record EVPs with has worked for me. I started out using an inexpensive Radio Shack model DR-85 handheld digital recorder. This was a great way for me to get started recording. Although the sound quality was not the best, it did serve the purpose. This is a great way to start. Cheap!

If you find yourself spending a lot of time recording and loading the files into a computer for analyzing, then you may want to invest in a more expensive recorder. The results will be better because you will hear more as the better recorder will have less "self noise" associated with it and it will capture finer details of the natural world around us.

My second recorder is a Sony that records in stereo and provides better sound quality than the Radio Shack model but does cost a whole lot more. It came with a CD with software so you can transfer and store your files via a USB cable into your computer. I have captured some really good EVPs from the cheap recorder and the same goes for the expensive one. The background noise is quieter with the Sony and therefore more satisfying for me, as hours are needed to analyze the data. So the differences may be small but both do a good job recording EVPs.

There is a school of thought out there that says the cheaper recorders work better because they provide internal noise to be used by the spirits to form words. Also, if you provide some noise like a TV turned to low volume, that would work, too. The same goes for signal generators using white, brown, or pink noise to give acoustical energy to the recording area. That does work, and so does silence. (White noise is a steady, unvarying, unobtrusive sound, as an electronically produced drone or the sound of rain, used to mask or obliterate unwanted sounds. It is random noise with a uniform frequency spectrum over a wide range of frequencies. Pink noise is a random signal with the audible frequency range whose amplitude decreases as frequency increases, maintaining constant audio power per frequency increment. Brown noise is similar to white noise, but at a lower frequency. Examples in nature include waves on the beach and some wind noise.)

I have to say that silence works best for me. I don't have to try to figure out what is being said because the recording area was quiet at the time. To eliminate all background noise and almost all human contamination is the best way to go. By human contamination I mean the less people in the recording area the better. People have found it difficult remaining quiet for long durations of time. And so if your equipment has almost no noise associated with it, then you will have nice clean EVPs to listen to, full of the richness of their voice and maybe some artifacts of where they are. The sound quality of an EVP should be of the utmost importance when you record. If you want to share them, there is nothing worse than to play a lot of noise and what might be someone saying something that is supposed to be an EVP.

Being somewhat of an audiophile, it was necessary for me to upgrade my recordings with better sound quality. This meant researching every possible way to record. I had a theory that a really good microphone, mixing board, and computer would get me what I wanted – and that is superior sound quality while still capturing EVPs. And it worked! I have 10 Studio Projects B3 condenser microphones, a Behringer Xenyx mixing board, and a Dell laptop computer with modern standard recording software. This set up allows me to place microphones in the rooms I want to record in and gives me the high fidelity I want. The system is nice and quiet and you can hear a pin drop from twenty-five feet away, clear as a bell. The EVPs? Clear, too. You can pick them out more easily because the nuances of their voices stand out above the people who are there during recording. They sound different, but not all the time.

To further the recording abilities it will be necessary to move to a multi-track recorder. This will allow you to record with all mics on at the same time and listen to all or any one track individually upon playback – thereby focusing on just where the EVP came from in the first place. Any digital recording system that has very high sound quality will be ideal, and to get any better may be just a matter of opinion of that sound quality.

A regular speaker can also be used to record with. Take a loud speaker and connect the leads so it will plug into the input of the microphone on your computer or other such recording device. It will become a large microphone, but it will not have as good a sound quality as a real microphone will have. It will also be limited in range for sound collection. But this, too, will work for collecting EVPs. Also, the speaker I used only has an effective recording range of about two feet. When listening to the playback of a file I made, the voice that was recorded sounds like it was coming from across the room which is impossible considering the range of the speaker. This kind of thing will have you scratching your heard over and over again as you record these strange phenomena for yourself.

The Spiricom and Spiritcom

There are also recording devices that fringe almost on disbelief. The Spiricom is a good example of this. Thomas Edison built one of these, supposedly, but no one has a blueprint of this device. If they did, they would be able to build his two-way communication device to the spirits. It is said that the government came in and took many of Edison's pieces of work and printed materials when he died. We will never know. However, that didn't stop people from experimenting and creating like devices that work as a two-way communication link.

George Meek and Bill O'Neil

Enter George Meek. George is a man who made a lot of money being a retired industrialist who had revolutionized the air conditioning industry. He also had a love of the paranormal.

He was able to accomplish the construction of the Spiricom along with the help of fellow researcher Bill O'Neil. This was a rather large device as it consisted of many tone generators in tune to the speaking male voice. They were able to make communication possible by just speaking and then listening to the voice come from the speaker in this machine.

Meek spent many hours in his large basement office piecing together roadmaps of the spirit worlds from the vast knowledge he had gained from his research. He had discovered that the actual locations of Heaven and Hell were not somewhere out there in distant space nor hidden away deep inside the Earth, but right here, all around us. He knew that mystics over the centuries have had an intimate knowledge of the fact that many universes interpenetrate our own physical universe, but they didn't know how to explain it to the world; humanity until now had always lacked the technological background to understand how this interpenetration worked. These universes are all jumbled together in the same space as they are sent out by God, yet each universe remains distinct by its frequency or rate of vibration.

The frequencies of the spirit worlds are much finer than the energies we are familiar with here on Earth, such as electricity, radio signals, and light. Most of these spirit-world energies are imperceptible not only by our physical senses, but also by modern scientific equipment.

In 1979, he and his colleague, Bill O'Neil, developed the Spiricom device, a set of thirteen tone generators spanning the range of the adult male voice. O'Neil was psychically gifted, and he collaborated with his spirit friends while developing the large radio-like apparatus, which gave off a droning buzz that filled the room. When O'Neil spoke in its presence, you could hear his voice getting wrapped up in the buzzing noises of the Spiricom machine. He worked on the machine for months, and then a most amazing thing happened. Another voice began to get wrapped up in the radio sounds, too—a voice belonging to someone who was present in the room, but invisible. The voice of a spirit.

George himself died in the winter of 1999, after circling the globe many times, acquiring undeniable proof of afterlife, and writing two pioneering books that opened up new markets and blazed the way for a new breed of writers on spiritual matters. George Meeks' two break-out books were, *Healers and the Healing Process*, published in the 1970s, and *After We Die, What Then?*, published in the 1980s.

The following is also an extract from the Inter Trans Communication web site:

> The spirit collaborator soon identified himself as Dr. George Jeffries Mueller, a NASA scientist who had died in 1967 and had now come close to the vibration of the Earth to assist Meek and O'Neil in opening a communication bridge between the two worlds. O'Neil and Mueller went on to record more than 20 hours of dialog between 1979 and 1982. In one dialog, Doc Mueller was giving O'Neil technical advice

Different Devices

on how to improve the Spiricom equipment:

"William, I think the problem is an impedance mismatch into that third transistor."

O'Neil replied slowly, as though studying the circuitry.

"Third transistor."

"Yes, the transistor that follows the input."

"I don't understand,"

replied O'Neil.

"The pre-amp, the pre-amp!" Doc Mueller stated emphatically.

"Oh, the pre-amp."

"Yes, I think that can be corrected by introducing a one-hundred-fifty-ohm, half-watt resistor in parallel with a point-double-oh-four-seven microfarad ceramic capacitor. I think we can overcome that impedance mismatch."

Obviously baffled, O'Neil lamented,

"Oh boy, I'll have to get the schematics."

This file is more easily understood when reading along with the script from the Internet. What an incredible sequence. So many people have witnessed this device in operation and must have been amazed hearing a voice coming across 13 tone generators!

Huge credit must be given to people like George Meek and Bill O'Neil. They have blazed the way for fellow researchers to unravel the mysteries that are abundant all around us. They had great success in building a device that opened communication into another world. This certainly is a fantastic starting point to anybody looking to do research in this field.

The Internet is a very important tool when gathering information about a subject that can be had no other way – except for going to the library and searching through many books on your particular subject, however that takes a very long time. When doing research into microphone building and their different applications, I stumbled across a web site about a unique man with a unique device. His name is Mike Dieser and like George Meek and Bill O'Neil he has built a Spiritcom.

This device works on different principles altogether, yet it to is a two-way spirit communication device. It is a more simple design due to the fact that Mike sees physics in his own way. He built

Different Devices

this device after reading a college-level physics book. Things made sense to him in the way he viewed acoustics and energy. His device uses the naturally occurring energy around the device as opposed to generating noise for the spirits to speak. Both of these devices do, however, make a fair share of noise. This is a result of electronics being used in a fashion a bit different than the way they are supposed to be used. However, the end result is the same: a door that has been opened to allow audible real-time communication with the unseen.

Mike Dieser and His Spiritcom in Action

I became fascinated as I combed over his web site looking for any information I could possibly find in order to build my very own Spiritcom. I began emailing Mike and asking questions on just how the device worked. Needless to say, he did not hand me the building instructions and owners manual. Instead, he gave me some experiments to perform so that I would learn just how acoustics behave and also the right mindset in engineering.

To think of building something from scratch, from an idea, and develop it into fruition was not something that I did on a regular basis. After

Spiritcom with parabolic sound collector.

performing experiments and having a lot of communication via e-mail, it was time for a telephone call to talk to him directly. Speaking to somebody really is the best way to communicate when exchanging ideas and asking numerous questions. He would ask me questions about the experiments I had performed and I had to continue answering him – and the only way to do this was to do the work, because there is no elevator to the top; you have to take the stairs. So after many months of emails and phone calls, a meeting took place. This meeting was to make me a partner in Spiritcom research, Mike Dieser's partner!

I was up for the task. After meeting him and seeing the Spiritcom he had built, I had the opportunity to hear this wonderful device in action. He fired it up after giving me full disclosure of just how it works and why. A male spirit did in fact come through; he spoke and then was gone. It was short lived but what a sound!

After gaining the understanding of how this Spiritcom worked, I went home to build my very own. The very next day, I completed a sort of make-shift unit just so I could get it working. Much to my delight, it sounded very much like Mike Dieser's Spiritcom. And it worked very well.

When I hooked up the unit, I was listening in on headphones and all of the sudden a woman sang about half of "Amazing Grace" to me! It was indeed amazing! My jaw actually dropped open in full wonderment. WOW! I only wish it came at a time when I could have recorded it. But that's okay, because I have a fantastic memory of the Spiritcom's potential.

Now all I had to do was to build a unit that was sturdy enough for field use. It needed to be able to take the abuse that Mike Dieser put his through. Although depending on how I built the inner workings would depend on how tough it could really be. After all, electronics don't like to be tossed around. That being said, Mike Dieser's Spiritcom was deliberately tossed in the back of his pick up truck and jostled around many times during research. And it still works fine. That shows his good engineering skills at work.

I am now in possession of one of his first units that has been used for years and torture tested. I am forever grateful to him for allowing me the opportunity to be his partner in Spiritcom research. My own experiments continue today with the device and will do so for years to come. It takes a lot of time to create something from scratch and then build it so that it works, especially in a field that is wide open as the paranormal.

Different Devices

Voices

Here are some files from Mike Dieser's Spiritcom.

This first one has the voice of a man saying,

```
"Beautiful dog."
```

[Play track 02]

There is a lot of noise associated with this device however we are working on improving the sound quality.

In this next clip you can hear Mike say,

"In the back?"

Then there is a voice of a man saying,

```
"'Really pissed me
over, I'm gonna fine
chill another wine."
```

[Play track 03]

You can hear the contrast between his voice and the EVP. This device certainly brings the voices up close into the recording! You would swear that it was someone in the room.

This last one is an eerily clear child saying,

```
"Hold on,
I want to talk."
```

[Play track 04]

He must be aware of the device and its capabilities.

It is results like these that drew me to Mike Dieser's work. Who wouldn't be intrigued? It is for that reason of excitement and intrigue that I wanted to join him in this research.

The following clip is from my own Spiritcom and you can very clearly hear a voice of a man say,

```
"Don't.
Talk a minute."
```

I respond with,

"That's a little better."

(After hearing it.)

And in the middle of those words, there is a female voice that says,

```
"I have to pee."
```

[Play track 05]

Frank's Box and the Shack Box

Frank Sumption is an electronic engineer and fellow EVP researcher. He has created a device that also allows for two-way communication and many call this device the telephone to the dead. Not ever building one from the schematics that Frank Sumption provides for free, I can only go on what he has told me and from what has been revealed over time on the internet and TV programs.

It works by using a car radio and an electronic sampling device that picks out small samples of the radio frequencies as it travels up and down the band widths. There is also a white noise generator adding sound to the radio signals. The end result is something that sounds much like the knob being turned fast on the radio. All this goes on automatically and there are adjustments that can be made to the device through knobs that can be turned on the control panel. Frank has made many of these boxes, and depending on which one you are listening to, you may or may not be hearing the same electronics as later models. Then it plays the little samples through a speaker so you can hear in real time the voices that spirits create using radio waves to communicate with. This has been called the answer to Edison's lost device, but I am sure, it too, is quite different. The voices are laid over the radio signals that are coming out of the speaker, meaning voices will appear over static, music, or the speaking voice of the DJ. The amazing thing with this device is that when you hear a voice speak a sentence that spans many frequency changes, you realize that it is not a DJ or anyone else on the radio—it is an EVP.

One may well argue the use of a radio to collect evidence of EVPs, however the answers to questions truly are something to think about. There is something about coincidence that just can't happen time and time again. I need to thank Frank Sumption for his dedication and engineering of a device that lends a great step forward into the field of paranormal research.

There is also a version of Franks Box that you can make at Radio Shack and is referred to as a Shack Box or the Radio Shack Hack. It works much the same as the Franks Box, and in using this device, I found the best way to get the most out of it is to record the session and then comb through the footage for the results. It is difficult to hear all the layers of data flowing through the speaker in real time. Listening to voices spanning many radio frequencies as they answer your questions is amazing, and this can only be paranormal in nature. The chances of all radio stations broadcasting a word in succession as the device scans all frequencies on the FM band so that it forms sentence structure is so statistically astronomical that you can effectively rule it out as the source of the voices.

The Shack Box also samples radio frequencies, only as it cruses up the AM or FM radio bands. It is not as refined as the Frank's Box, but it still works and the results are almost the same.

I had the opportunity to see just how this device works when investigating a house in Wareham Massachusetts. The messages come in quite fast and a trained ear will be able to pick out the voices in a more steady fashion as compared to the voices that may be coming from the broadcaster. You can hear small clips from the radio stations as the device scans up and down AM and FM frequencies. Again, the more training you give your ear, the more easily these voices will stand out. You must have patience.

The following clip is from that investigation and this device belongs to Tim Weisberg from *Spooky South Coast* radio. Tim is a seasoned paranormal investigator and his experience shows when doing investigations with him. We had gone into the attic and started asking questions using the Shack Box.

Tim asks,

"What is your name please?"

and the voice in an uncharacteristic sound quality of the device says,

`"Kelly."`

[Play Track 06]

Listen to the clarity of the voice and its strength. This is strange since it came out of a very small speaker and doesn't sound like the normal voices on the radio.

Also, there is another spirit answering and he says,

`"I don't…I don't know."`

This small passage spans almost 40 frequency changes as they speak.

Garbage in, garbage out. Use the best equipment you can afford. Quality first.

The quieter the recording system, the clearer the EVPs will be.

Shut up! Shut up! Shut up!

This next clip of the Shack Hack is long at twenty-three seconds but it shows a certain regularity with communication. Even though the voice is somewhat methodical in its occurrence the radio does not repeat a complete cycle of the FM band within the time frame of this communication. It almost seems like there is interference when the voice speaks.

See if you can hear a male EVP shout,

"Shut up!"

three times.

[Play track 07]

If you use a Spiritcom, Frank's Box, a Shack Box, or a cheap handheld recorder, it will work. I believe it isn't what you use to record with, but how you use it. By that, I think you have to believe in what you are doing. Take the stance of truly believing that you will capture EVPs and not one of doubt and disbelief. I think this will improve your chances of recording the unseen voices. Try to connect with the unknown and they will come through for you.

If you want to try to make one of these inexpensive paranormal toys, there is a small alteration that you must make in order for the radio to work as a scanning device. You have to open the back of the radio, remove two screws that hold down the schematic board, and cut the connection that says "mute." Then put the schematic board back in place and tighten the screws down holding it in place. Now re-attach the back panel. Tim Weisberg uses the Radio Shack model 12 - 469. There is another model, the 12 -470, which works just as well, but requires a bit more work to make it functional and has a speaker. The model 12-469 does not have a speaker. You can find video directions on every step needed on the web site UFO geek.com.

(Please note that these directions do not specifically endorse or negate any electronic product used for these purposes nor the readjustment or tampering of said product. You do so at your own expense and risk. If you do choose to use these directions and you are not able to understand the mechanics, please find someone to help you.)

And a *Word* With You, Please...

Another method in capturing EVPs is leaving your computer on with the Word program open to a new document. Before you go to bed ask several questions and just let the spirits type out their responses. This works, but may take some time so don't give up. People have received strange messages that have come in through fax machines as well, and the same method applies of asking questions and waiting.

Voicemail Experiment

Voicemail is yet another way to record EVPs. Ask the spirit to please leave you a message on your voicemail and say the number aloud so they will know which number to use. Now, this sounds a bit crazy, but it works and I have done exactly that. While at work around noon time for several days in a row, I thought of my work phone number very hard in my mind. I was trying to project my thoughts into the spirit realm to see if I could get a response. This is based on my theory that everything we think and feel is flowing from our minds into the air and beyond into different dimensions, most importantly the spirit world. I repeated my request for someone to contact me at my work phone number and spoke the numbers in my mind over and over for a good ten to fifteen minutes. That's a long time if you were to try this for yourself, but don't give up. Try it for several days and see what happens.

About two weeks later I had a message on my voicemail which is part of my normal day at work and I was very surprised when I dialed the number. The message was fast and short. My experiment had yielded results. Wow, was I surprised! It worked. A few days later another message was left on my voicemail and I couldn't believe it! Someone must have been listening to my mind and proved my theory – well, at least to me, anyway. This is an extraordinary personal experience and I hope it works for you as well.

The following recordings have been taken directly from my voicemail using a small microphone pressed up to the speaker on the telephone so the sound quality may be lacking.

The next clip sounds like a young woman's voice saying,

"Call me kid."

[Play track 08]

This is the entire message and is somewhat surprising because it's just a one to two second recording. It's as though someone dialed my number, then changed their mind, didn't say anything, and then hung up the phone. In the time from when the connection was initially made to the hanging up, there was only a very short time span. I believe an EVP popped into the only opportunity it had at that time. Did a spirit really dial my voicemail and leave me a message? Maybe they do by proxy. Or they really do have the ability to control energy in this fashion which would explain the ability to leave written messages on a computer without actually typing out the words.

Another message left on my voicemail is also of a woman. This time the message

is not one of levity but one of a cry for help. We, as human beings, hear the word *help* and most of us will help the one asking for it. It's our nature to help one another, but when you hear someone ask for help and there is nothing you can do, your only choice is to ignore their plea. I have recorded spirits asking for help and this is actually a fairly common request, not just for me but for other people who record EVPs as well.

Do spirits need help? Maybe they do, which would make them more like human beings than we know.

The next clip has two voices in it. It starts with someone quickly whispering,

```
"Can I..."
```

and another voice that is louder, saying,

```
"Please help."
```

[Play track 09]

How can I help a voice on the phone in a message? It's a bit distressing hearing it and leaves one feeling somewhat helpless themselves. There are different scenarios that may be involved here and you can easily make one work to explain the communication in the recording. Possibly, one spirit may be asking for something from the one who is trying to leave the message – just like a child interrupts you as you are trying to leave a message on someone else's voicemail. Or, it may be that the energy increased halfway through the spoken message going from a whisper to more rich in character much like our own voices.

The next recording is even more unusual. When I listened to the message I had a hard time trying to figure out what was being said. It seemed like it was spoken in reverse.

I will first play the track in its original form so you may understand the way it sounds.

[Play track 10]

It too is only a second or two long in duration and spoken quite fast and is unintelligible.

Here is the exact same track played in reverse.

[Play track 11]

Now it makes more sense as a name appears:

```
Patrick Anderson.
```

I've never heard of this person, nor do I know if they work for the same company that I do. The speed in which it was left on my machine is not the way people speak on the phone, so it is unusual to say the least.

And their may also be another voice imbedded in this message.

Listen for

"Call Rick"

in a woman's voice.

It is difficult to hear, but appears in the very beginning of the recording. It is almost as though they were making the most of the time allotted to them, so more than one spirit spoke.

My Own Device

Have you ever heard of Instrumental Transcommunication or ITC for short? It is a method of using video recorders and other electronic devices like short wave radios in building other devices in order to communicate. George Meek built his Spiricom using an array of tone generators and amplifiers. The device opened up a two-way communication window. There are people making like devices today.

After hearing about the Frank's Box, I wanted to build one of my own, but it would have to be my way, as I did not understand the schematics Frank Sumption provided – after all I am not an electrical engineer. But I did, however, build my version of a two-way communication device.

The result was a very simple device that incorporated a short wave radio and a microphone. This recording was made shortly after I hooked it up.

It is a woman saying,

"I hear you, in Plymouth."

[Play track 12]

It's a strange way to speak, but she gets her point across. I must point out that I live near Plymouth, Massachusetts, and I was spending a lot of time on Burial Hill recording EVPs at the time. So when this woman came through with her message, I believed her! I was there asking questions and moving in and around the grave markers, usually at night, and she was there, too. That's what I got out of it. This was a strange coincidence, or was it? That's one thing to wonder about the spirit world, are there any coincidences? Maybe this is all meant for a reason?

Strange Experiments

People who experiment with EVPs often get very creative as in a technique of using a candle or other flame source and photoelectric cells. As sound travels across the flame and/or through it, the photoelectric cell picks up on the difference of intensity the flame produces and transforms it into sound. I am sure there is a computer in this set up somewhere, but what a very unique method of recording.

As research in this field keeps getting weirder and more fascinating every day, the closer we are getting to the perfect device. Someday, someone will discover the method of a constant direct line of communication with the other dimensions revealing to mankind once and for all just where we are headed.

Surely someone on that side knows?

My term for altered or stolen acoustics: *Acoustical Energy Remodulation*. This means a spirit can reshape sound and communicate using that same energy. They can take all or part of it, and they know when a sound will occur.

Normal movement from people in the room provides enough acoustic energy for a spirit to transform it into words, listen carefully.

EVPs can be recorded low in frequency with a sentence spread out over time. They also can be only a word or two spoken very fast and high in frequency. And then there is everything else in between.

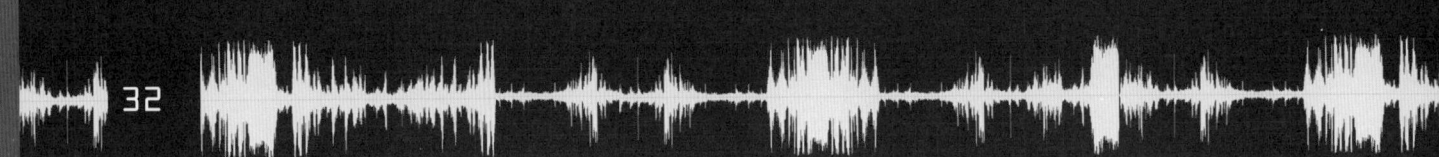

2

My Beginning: This Old House

In 1997, my wife and I saw a large one-room school house that would turn into a lovely home if we could do most of the renovations ourselves. We approached a local real estate company for information on the property. We were looking for a fixer upper with a lot of character because to me they were just more interesting. It turned out that the schoolhouse needed too much work, but the real estate agent said she would call us if anything came up—and she did, one year later. A friend of hers had just passed away and the family was going to sell a house; and would I be interested?

We weren't really looking at that time, but my wife agreed to take a look at it, so we made an appointment. It was a smaller house, but was shaded by a large tree next to the road that hung its branches over the front yard as well. It looked old, but did it have the character on the inside? We went in and saw character alright, from the 70s! Complete with lime green sink and bathtub. Nice linoleum parquet flooring, too. But the living room had nice dark hardwood floors and nice back to back fireplaces. We'll take it.

After speaking with the previous owners, we found out the house was built circa 1830 and the wood was most likely used from a mill that existed during the same time. Maybe the trees from property were used in its construction? It is a possibility as that was a common practice back then. Also, remember the realtor whose friend had died and the house went up for sale? I was speaking to her son and found out that she'd died of cancer in the house! So I asked, "Do you think the house is haunted?" He said, "Yes. There appears to be the spirit of an old lady here who doesn't like the curtains in the living room and many times we found that they are on the floor. We just can't seem to keep them up. I guess she doesn't like them."

We found out, later, that there was more than one spirit that haunted this home. At this point in time, though, I

This Old House 33

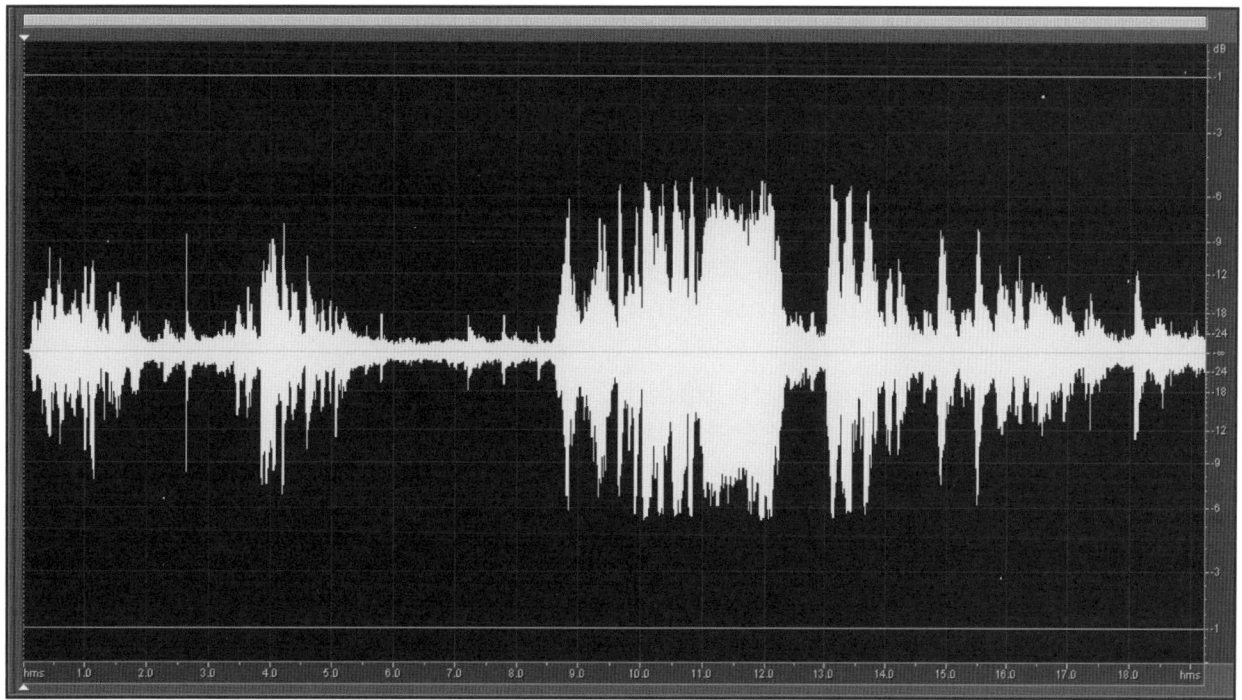

TRACK 13: You can clearly see just when the woman screams in the middle of the screen as a solid mass of sound makes an unbroken decibel signature.

wasn't into the paranormal world too much. It wasn't until I started watching *Ghost Hunters* on TV that my interest really perked up. But on one mild Halloween night, in 2004, a friend was having a party. Outside, a small crowd had gathered and another friend of mine, Jordie, was passing around a set of headphones. The people listening were ripping them off and yelling in surprise.

Wanting to know what was up, I asked what they were listening to. Jordie then gave me the headphones and pressed play on her micro cassette recorder. I too was amazed at what I heard. She told me it was a ghost she had recorded during a walk through of a historic home in Duxbury, Massachusetts.

The recording plays like this:

During the tour she and a friend passed a table in the dining room, commenting on how you shouldn't touch anything. Then a scream is heard. A woman screams,

"Get out!"

in the kind of blood curdling scream that is typical of any horror movie.

[Play track 13]

My Beginning:

However, it was not heard by anyone at the time of the recording. I asked for her to play it again. The scream penetrated my brain like a slug from a .45. I knew at that moment that I wanted to record EVPs. What a thrill! A spark had been lit inside of me that would only grow in the years to come.

The next day, I ran down to Radio Shack and purchased a DR-85 digital recorder. Ever since then, I immediately began getting EVPs. There was no break in period for me, just full steam ahead. A day or two after the purchase, I got started. I had heard of a technique of turning on the TV and turning the volume down low to give acoustic energy into the room. This is supposed to aid in the EVPs being able to highjack the energy for their voices to form. I remember the Anna Nicole Show was on and my wife was half a sleep on the couch. I didn't think she'd mind if the volume was turned down. I was wrong, but she let me record anyway. I am glad she did because I captured my first Class A EVP!

[Class A recordings are those that do not need any processing to hear what is being said. Class B recordings may require headphones to hear clearly and they are less easily understood. Sometimes mild filtration can remove background noise enough as to allow for EVP clarity. Class C recordings need processing, like filtering, in order to understand what is being said. People will have a difference of opinion when listening to this class of recordings. I have added Class D to this scale and I describe it as high frequency whispering. I do this because those types of voices make up most of the recordings I have. Most people have a hard time hearing them, if at all. Practice is needed to allow your brain to recognize this Class D category that fringes upon periodolia.]

As I mentioned, I used the idea of turning the volume on the TV to low and then recorded to see what happened. This is supposed to put acoustic energy into the area you wish to record in.

The voice I captured was a woman who told me,

"F*****g cold"

right into the microphone in a loud whisper!

[Play track 14]

The recording sent the hairs up on my arms and neck and an electrical charge up my spine. This came from my house! It creeped me out a bit at first, but you learn to readjust your fear levels if you wish to pursue recording EVPs. I was excited and wanted more. This was so new to me and I didn't understand how this could happen. I played the recording for my friend, Jordie, and her eyes bolted open as she used expletives at what she was hearing.

I did, too, to tell you the truth. I mean it's hard to believe it when you record an EVP for the first time but can't explain it. You just tell your self that it's only a ghost. But is that any solace? The recording basically confirms you have a haunted house, doesn't it? But everything appeared to be quite normal to me in our home. Yes, it's an old house, but it seemed to be peaceful.

BOOO to You!

Now that *Ghost Hunters* was airing and certain friends of mine were also watching it, Jordie wanted to form our own group to investigate paranormal activity. If they can do it, why can't we? She got several people together who were also friends who had this special interest in common and so formed the Boston Organization for Odd Occurrences or B.O.O.O. for short. We had two sensitives, a historian, and an EVP guy – me. We even had someone using dowsing rods for question and answer sessions. There were digital cameras for gathering photos, video cameras, tape recorders, and handheld digital recorders. Plus a whole lot of humor. We would go to restaurants after investigating to replenish ourselves from ghost hunting. It is a theory that your energy can be taken from you as you immerse yourself into paranormal situations. Those days are some of the best of my life and will be forever grateful for true friendship.

Over the years, we gathered tons of evidence, including hundreds of orb data on video. Some extraordinary ones at that! The EVPs numbered in the hundreds and then thousands! As time went by, I purchased a laptop computer in order to keep the recordings permanent and analyze the data. A computer is a necessary piece of equipment if you want to store all your files and replay them. I would also recommend an external hard drive for back up.

These next recordings were taken in my home and a male voice seems to be there quite often during that time. This clip was made using the Radio Shack DR-85 digital recorder.

It is a male spirit saying,

"He's going all the way."

[Play track 15]

You can hear the reverb as he speaks which is not a condition of the room. There is carpeting, a couch, and a large chair with an ottoman. There are also curtains (that are staying up) on the sides of the windows. So where is the reverb coming from? Maybe from his side of wherever he is at the time he spoke? I now wonder if this is a prophetic message about me? If I go all the way with paranormal investigating, does that mean that I will be on TV too like the *Ghost Hunters* or maybe I'll write a book? My decision was not based on that recording by the way but it's funny how things turn out.

In those early days of recording, I used the TV technique often as I had gotten results with it in previous recording sessions. This next clip is from one of those and the TV was turned down low as I sat on the edge of the couch, waiting in anticipation as to what voices would be heard.

This one has the reverb again and is simple in nature as he simply says,

> "Hi"

– but in a sing song fashion.

[Play track 16]

You will hear it at the end of the recording. The TV was on to give that energy to the room when this was recorded. The voice sounds almost robotic, doesn't it? And that's the thing about EVPs: They are not always going to be in the condition you might think, like a clear-speaking voice. There are going to be artifacts to the voices like reverb or echo.

In the case of this next EVP, it is loud but not too clear on what he is saying. It may be the name Thomas Straight? Or Tom is straight or even Tom has strength. You decide.

[Play track 17]

This male spirit seems to be directing me to take care of the walkway by saying,

> "Why don't you clear your walkway?"

[Play track 18]

The only thing that I can think of regarding a walkway is next to my bed. I have stacks of magazines, books, and computer screen prints that I have for research, along with scattered electronic equipment, speakers, and wires.

I don't like to record much in my house because I want it to be a neutral zone of paranormal activity, so I have somewhere to escape to. I don't want to turn my home into a spiritual hot spot. Although sometimes you won't make a difference no matter what you do, they are here to stay.

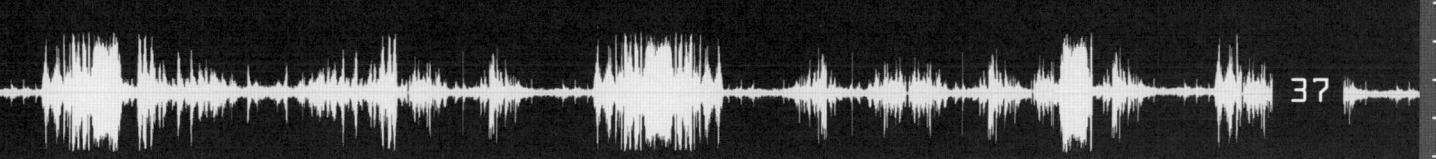

3

Old Duxbury House
Duxbury

Our group had the incredible opportunity to investigate a real haunted house right from the beginning. The owners were also interested in the paranormal, so it was a great match up. Because the owners have professional jobs, they wish to remain anonymous, so no information will be given as to their names or the whereabouts of the house. B.O.O.O. had spent a great deal of time in this place and we've gathered a great deal of paranormal evidence as well. I don't believe I've ever spent so much time investigating any one location as I have this one and I thank the owners for allowing me to record there.

The first time I entered the house I could feel pressure pushing down upon me and the air seemed to be filled with static electricity. This was the sort of place that you would almost expect to be haunted. It is lavishly decorated with period furniture and also has many authentic paintings on the walls. You would almost expect to see people walking around the house as they would have in the early 1800s. When you have the ocean just a stones throw away, the smell of the salt air combined with well-manicured grounds, and a haunted house, I can tell you, there is no place I'd rather be!

But I think, after all the investigating, I can say that this place truly is haunted. It has never let me down. All the times I have been there, I have walked away with many, many EVPs. I have recorded the same voice several times on different investigations, and some of the best recordings I have came from this house.

One of the things you can do with the data you collect is draw conclusions based on the evidence. It may be factual, or it may not be, but there it is nonetheless, to be evaluated.

This next clip is that of a man saying,

The Old Duxbury House

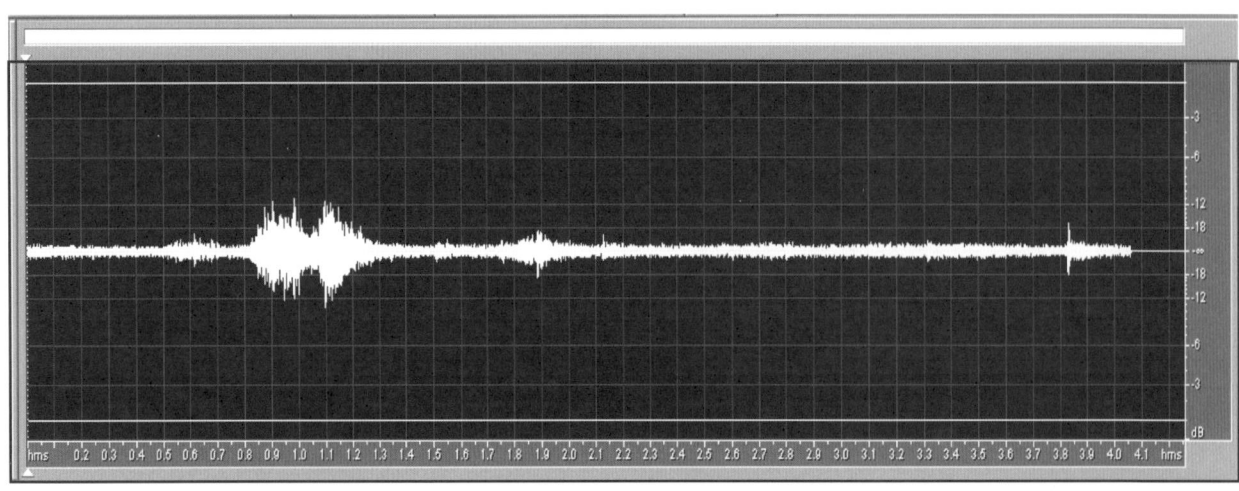

Track 20. The whip of energy that denotes "Here we go!" can clearly be seen on this Cool Edit decibel meter.

`"Damn hot."`

[Play track 19]

If you lived in Duxbury in the middle of the summer in the 1800s, yes, I guess it would be damn hot without air conditioning. So is this a truth brought to light by a spirit? It may very well be in this example, however, you can't always trust what people say in this life or the next. People don't always tell the truth. And for those who believe that what they are saying is factual, it may indeed be false. There are also different ways of looking at something. Take "Damn hot" for instance. Is the temperature really hot or is the spirit speaking about one of the investigators being damn hot as in sexy?

This next clip involves more than one voice in different volumes and style of speaking.

The first voice of a male says,

`"Get out"`

spoken very fast, but loud, followed by someone saying,

`"Here we go."`

This was spoken in a fast, but loud, voice.

Then a female says in a quiet whisper,

`"Shut the front door."`

She speaks softly but with headphones you will be able to hear her speak clearly.

[Play track 20]

I have been told that the female voice may be saying a swear word, which is something different than what I hear. But this will always be the case with EVPs, as different people will often hear different things. This clip is a good example of how intense a voice can be recorded as well as how softly. You can hear my footsteps in the recording as the digital audio recorder picks up almost all the sounds around you.

The following clip is a spirit of a woman that has been recorded several times inside the house.

In this recording you can hear her clearly say,

"No thank you."

Or she may also be saying

"Don't thank me."

[Play track 21]

This is an odd phenomenon. As I mentioned, different people are going to hear different things on EVPs recordings. It may have to do with how the brain interprets the information given to it. Someone may hear three syllables and yet someone else may hear five.

Another strange phenomenon is reversing files to get data. In this case she is saying,

"We can't go home."

[Play track 22]

This is the exact same track as #21, only reversed.

Reversing a track playing it backwards: Most computers come with a basic recording program called "Sound Recorder." From the bottom of your computer screen, click on *start, all programs, accessories, entertainment* than *sound recorder*. [This is the path on my Dell PC and may need to be adjusted for varied computers.] Insert a microphone into the microphone input on your computer, then a red circle on the program will pop up. This is the record button. The black rectangle means stop; use the double arrow left to rewind the recording. Use the single arrow pointing right to play. (These are very easy controls to use and it doesn't take much practice to master.) Here is where the reversing of a track comes in. So let's say you have recorded a track and want to play it in reverse, click on *effects,* then *reverse*. This will reverse the file so you can play it backwards. Click on *effects,* then *reverse* to play it forwards again.

Now back to the track—what can we derive from what she is saying? She uses the word "we" spoken in the plural, not singular as in I. She is not alone. She can't go home? Does that mean she died away from her home or that she can't reach Heaven where home truly is, making her trapped in the spaces in between?

The next clip is a cheerful one of a male saying,

"Warm wishes."

[Play track 23]

You will hear the camera chime then the voice follows. It was nice to hear this message as it affirms that there are nice people there, too.

Another somewhat warm message is found in the next clip of a man saying,

"Where'd the dog been?"

[Play track 24]

This file is uncharacteristic in the strength of the EVP as it usually appears, in a typical recording, much lower in volume. There was controversy among the group over the nature of its authenticity. Pictures were found that the homeowners provided us to look at, and there was one picture of a man standing at the front door with a dog beside him. In the clip, I wonder if he means it from the viewpoint that the dog had run away and now it has returned, or the dog died, too, and is now reunited with his owner? We'll never know.

Here is another warm wish for those of us upon entering the house.

You can hear one of the investigators say,

"Paula, have you been here?"

Paula replies,

"Uh uh"

as the back door is opened and we enter. On top of that noise, right at the beginning, you can here a male voice say,

"Come forward."

[Play track 25]

It's like he is welcoming us into the home, as though he was actually there – and he very well may have been there. It sure seems that way by this recording. This voice is laid over the sound of the doorknob turning just as we enter the kitchen through the back door. This kind of overlay is very common when they communicate. The theory goes that sometimes a spirit needs more energy than they can produce, so they highjack sound to form their own words. This may very well be the case because I have many recordings that support this theory. They ride the wave of acoustic energy as they form words which gives their voice the same pattern as the original sound. If the frequency rises in pitch so too does their voice, and the same goes for the opposite direction in low frequency.

But like all things paranormal, they are not locked into this way of speaking. Sometimes this method will be applied, but their voice will remain steady without the original sound changing the voice at all. Maybe, with all the options of speaking available to them, it becomes more a matter of choosing the way they want to speak and not so much by using any applied law or principle they need to follow.

In this next recording you will here a spirit calling out the name of one of our investigators Patrick. Patrick is asking about the woman who seems to haunt the home.

"We'd like to know who the woman is who is trying to communicate."

Our psychic picks up on the spirit yelling Patrick's name and makes a comment that,

'Someone's screaming. A woman is screaming when you said that."

[Play track 26]

You can here a female yelling

"Patrick"

three times in a loud whispery voice. Why is she trying to get his attention? Does she want to warn him about something? Also, no one heard this woman yelling Patrick's name except our psychic who picked right up on it. Not even Patrick who the spirit was yelling at. I never was too interested in psychics or mediums but I now know that there are certain people who really have this talent as this clip demonstrates.

The last clip from this house is one of me saying,

"...would not be seen by most people in the world."

I think I was referring to the preservation of one of the paintings in the home. Following that, you hear a male voice say,

"Yeah."

It has a deep character to it and no one in the group has that deep of voice.

[Play track 27]

This is only a small sample of EVPs collected from this beautiful old house. Sometimes when you collect this many clips, you can put history together in a way never before thought possible. By actually finding history, after the fact, you can provide validity to what the voices are speaking about. However, in old houses, such as this, it may not be possible – as in the sad recording I got of a possible rape situation. The voice of a man says,

"Push her down."

And upon reversing the file it says,

"Remove her shirt."

It is a theory that reverse speech will directly have something to do with what is being spoken forwards. If this is the case here, then this may be insight to something horrible that happened a long time ago and the chances of that being printed in a newspaper or found in some historical record is next to impossible. If in fact this occurred in this house at all. Maybe there are visitors floating from house to house committing crimes in the world of spirit?

Visual and Sound Anomalies

Whatever the case may be, this house has given me and the BOOO crew valuable information into the study of the paranormal. The light anomalies that have been caught on video cameras, although this is a different area than EVPs, is well worth mentioning here as we have captured many unexplained orbs floating all around us as we investigate. There are dozens of exceptional orbs that may require more study in the future.

There are also the sounds of knocks, growls, strange scrapping and all together odd occurrences that would occur so frequently that it cannot be just coincidence. There is even the account of a grand father clock that began working in fast forward, then stopped for no apparent reason. The weights that control the workings had been disabled as the owners did not want to wear it out due to its age. This was actually witnessed by a BOOO member.

It is my hope that someday this invaluable location may be open to the public for paranormal investigations with the help from its current owners.

4

The First Church Weymouth

**17 Church Street,
Weymouth Heights, MA 02189**

Once again history plays an important role in one of the oldest churches in the country. How could it not? The following information is an excerpt taken from a historical web site about the church.

The First Church in Weymouth, Massachusetts (United Church of Christ) was first gathered in 1623. In that same year, settlers arrived accompanied by Reverend William Morrell who was a rector of the Church of England, who remained for just over a year. Reverend Mr. Barnard took over from 1624 until 1635. The church existed in only a provisional way from 1635 to 1639 during which time a great deal of religious dissension took place. The people of Weymouth joined in covenant on January 30, 1639 as peace and unity was finally achieved in 1644 with the arrival of Reverend Thomas Thatcher, from then until the establishment of the south precinct or parish in 1723, the town was all one precinct.

This church has a somewhat unusual history attached to it, one of many deaths. At least that's what local legend has to offer. The story goes that way back in the early 1800s, an angry priest had taken the Sunday school children into the basement and made them kneel down and pray for their sins. As the children prayed, he left the room, locking the door behind him. He then proceeded to light the entire church on fire with the children still inside. What an incredibly distressing story this is. The priest must

The eerily haunted First Church in Weymouth, Massachusetts.

have been disturbed beyond help to have done such a thing, if it happened at all. But this particular church has been burned down several times, only to be rebuilt. It does make you wonder.

Another tale involves the cemetery right next door. The tale tells of grave markers that were removed to make way for the expansion of the parking area. And as anyone knows, this can't be good.

B.O.O.O. had gained access to the church one evening while a *Jazzercise* class was going on in the basement room at the very back of the building. The side door was open to allow the participants of the class to come and go as they pleased. We decided to enter the church in two small groups. I would be included in both groups since I would be doing the recording. There is a recent story of someone we know who saw a black figure in the doorway, chasing them out. Our friend was horrified at the site of this entity and the

"Get out!"

it yelled at him! So when we entered the door, we were a bit apprehensive, but we went on.

The following was recorded when we first entered the building in the small hallway before you either go downstairs to the basement or go upstairs to the back of the sanctuary. You will hear the small boom box playing music in the background. Someone tries to warn us by saying,

"Watch out."

Then a loud male whisper, almost a speaking voice, says,

"What the f*** is this?"

[Play track 28]

He says this is a sing song fashion. Is this the priest who burned down the first church with the children still inside? Maybe he stays in the church to ask for forgiveness? What a thing for a spirit to say in a church, even if it's not the priest! That recording brings up interesting conversations when I play it for fans of EVPs. It also brings up theories on just how an angry foul-mouthed spirit can exist in a house of God.

The recording continues and a woman's voice sings way above the volume of the boom box. The voice obviously is not coming from the boom box. She also speaks in a sing-song fashion,

"Yes she says, she sings, she is safe."

This is truly an incredible recording. There is a woman speaking of another

46 The First Church

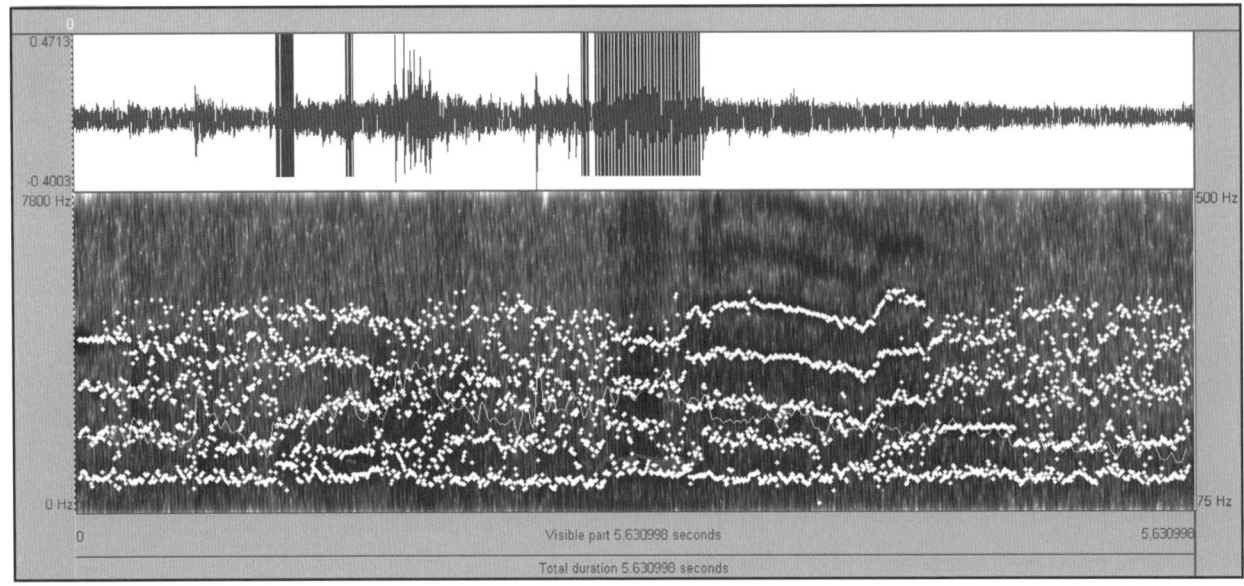

TRACK 29: There is a lot of information on this screen shot, but it helps to solidify that this is a human speaking voice. Notice the small diamond shapes, which are called formants, appear tightly grouped together. This is characteristic of a human speaking voice. There are also pulses that show in the top half of the screen print as vertical lines that all speaking human beings have.

woman or girl being safe and she is singing.

These EVPs are almost too perfect and seem to fit the legend all to well but if I didn't record it for myself, I may not believe it.

This next clip from the haunted church was recorded from the sanctuary.

I asked,

"Are there any children here?"

and about twenty seconds later, the following child's voice was recorded.

[Play track 29]

I can't really understand just what is being said but the clarity of the voice in the recording still gives me chills when I hear it. There is also the sound of a lens from digital camera moving.

These recordings are thought provoking to say the least. It is investigations like this one that makes this work so appealing. You just don't expect the results to be so good sometimes. But when they are, it doesn't get any better than this! If you are interested, the church is still located at 17 Church Street.

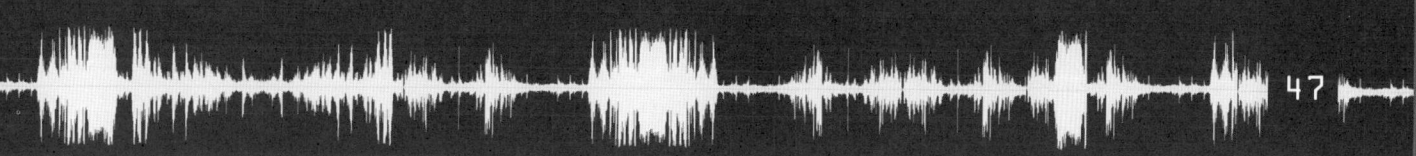

5

The North Church Hingham

**1 Lincoln Street
Hingham, MA 02043**

The very old North Church in Hingham, Massachusetts.

Ancient tombs submerged in the hill side.

In 1805 there was only one meeting house in North Hingham, the old North Meeting House, now known as the Old Ship Church.

As you approach the graveyard from the left of the church, there is a large iron gate. You can enter by going around the granite pylons where it leads you right to the row of tombs. These go back to the 1700s and are quite impressive as far as tombs go. They have the look of old Boston carved into the markers and in the brick work that binds them together. They are built into the hillside and are a must see when visiting.

This cemetery has unique structural features built into it, like the graves that line a small hillside that faces the street. It also has several circular plots and many statues. This is a very pretty cemetery

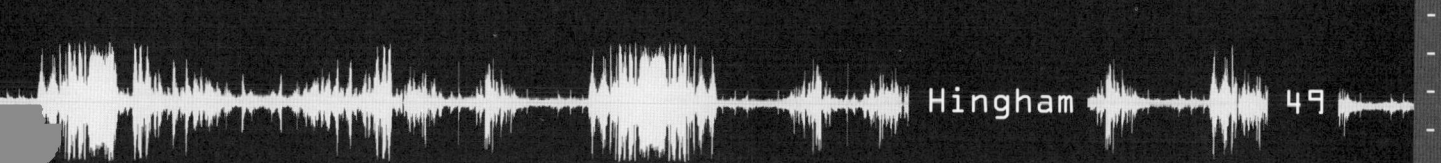

The pearly gates of the North Church cemetery.

and worth a stroll to admire the handy work from past centuries.

The EVPs that I have from this location do not number in the many of class A examples. But one night, a male EVP came through loud and clear and has an interesting twist to it.

Here he is saying,

```
"Playin' poker,
   important."
```

[Play track 30]

The twist is that this is not the way it was recorded. You must reverse the file if you want to hear the way it was originally recorded.

The North Church

[Play Track 31]

This is an example of reverse speech which means there are sentences spoken in reverse during normal forward speaking. It becomes apparent when you play the file backwards.

This is a great place to visit at night under a full moon as there are many layers to explore and just as many turns, creating a sense that you are in a special place. I have ventured into this old cemetery many times with different groups of people and the recordings that come from it are more of the whispery kind. There seems to be a lot of low volume chatter going on here and I need to spend more time recording at this site.

Use the software that came with your recorder to transfer files into your computer. Using a USB cable is much more efficient and will lessen the noise of the preamp if you were to use the headphone jack plugged into the microphone input to transfer files.

6
Cordage Park Plymouth

One of the many run down buildings of Cordage Park.

Cordage Park

A haunted house made of cement.

Cordage Park is a mysterious place. The enormous buildings nearest the entrance where the shops are located still echo of the days of old where rope was made that was to be used all over the world. There are even pieces of machinery that were purposefully left during reconstruction to remind us all of the once-important thriving business that supported so many lives.

There are a lot of outbuildings that have been abandoned over the years, and to walk through the site, you get the feeling that you're walking back in history. One can just imagine the busy workers making rope for the world out of this factory. These abandoned buildings are not to be explored because they appear to be dangerous, they have not been kept up over the years. If you want

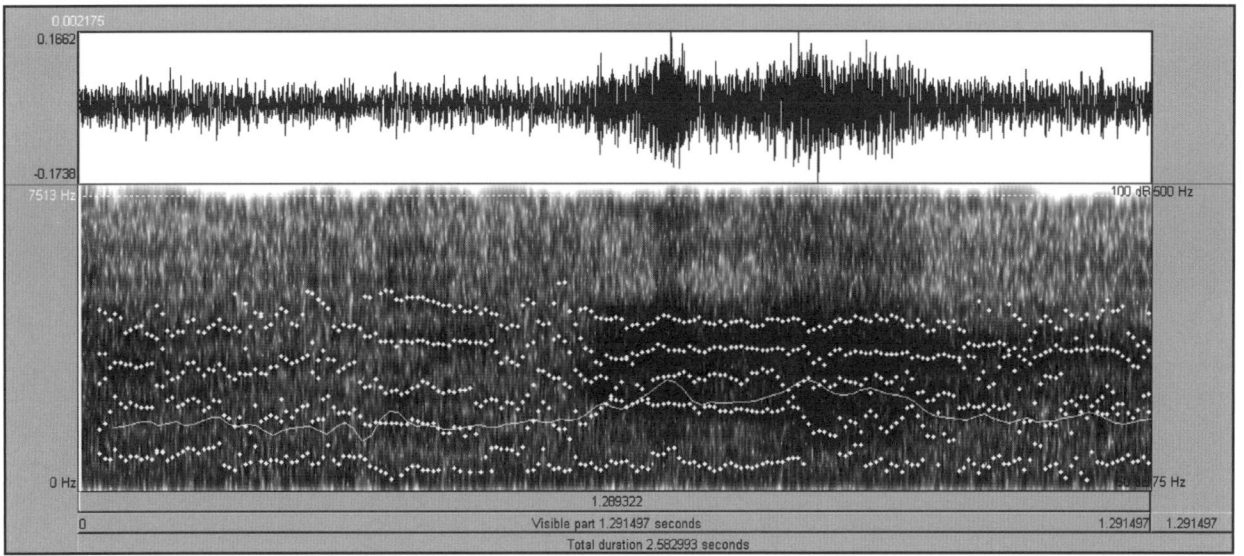

Track 32 (Chapter 6) Notice the small diamonds come together and become regular when the spirit speaks. Also, the intensity is apparent by the darkened background which shows decibel strength.

to investigate them, I would proceed with caution and **only so with the permission of the building owners**. B.O.O.O. did not go into these buildings at all because it was at night and we did not want to risk anybody getting hurt which is a good lesson when investigating.

You should always visit the site in the day before going in at night. That way you know to what expect when you are investigating in the dark.

My group walked down to the pier and entered a cement building which, at the time, was safe to enter. This building was made entirely out of cement and the acoustics inside were much like that of a church, with a lot of reverb. We were not expecting to see any ghosts or to pick up any EVPs, however, I did manage to capture several very good audio clips. The reason for this is, I assumed, is that the building looked too new to contain any real history. But that didn't mean it didn't have its fair share of spirits, as I found out when reviewing the audio files.

The first good EVP that I recorded there was this one saying,

"Get out! Go back!"

[Play track 32]

I played it for the group and we all were excited to hear it. It's a very clear whisper with a bit of strength to it. But why tell us to get out? The place was completely empty except for a cast iron spiral staircase in the corner. Why the haste to remove us from an otherwise empty building? We don't know.

The long row of connected buildings where rope was made.

Here's another warning to leave the building.

In the recording, you will hear one of the investigators speaking and on top of her voice you can hear a loud whispery voice say,

"Go back, behind you."

The investigator says,

"It's got a real cozy...can I borrow that flashlight?"

[Play track 33]

Is there a spirit there that someone does not want us associating with? I have had messages like that before, so maybe this is the case, too?

Through the gloomy messages I was picking up a ray of light in the recording of,

"One teacher."

[Play track 34]

What a nice message when taken in the good sense. This, too, is a loud whispery voice and may be the same lingering spirit as in the previous clips. It is hard to distinguish between different spirits when this kind of cadence is all you have to go on.

Maybe this place is visited and not maintained by any spirits. I say this because I cannot see how a child would stay there. This clip shows again the interaction between children and adults. Clearly we take care of our young ones in the afterlife just like we do now.

This recording is an excellent one in that it has three different people speaking. The first is a loud whisper that says,

"Patrick."

In between a man says,

"I don't think so."

And the third is that of a child saying,

"We warned you."

Even the kids are warning us about this place.

[Play track 35]

Maybe there was someone else there that would do us harm? There always seems to be more questions than answers.

Listen for voices carried on the sound of a breeze, blowing through a screen door.

7

Fort Revere Hull

60 Farina Road
Hull, MA 02045

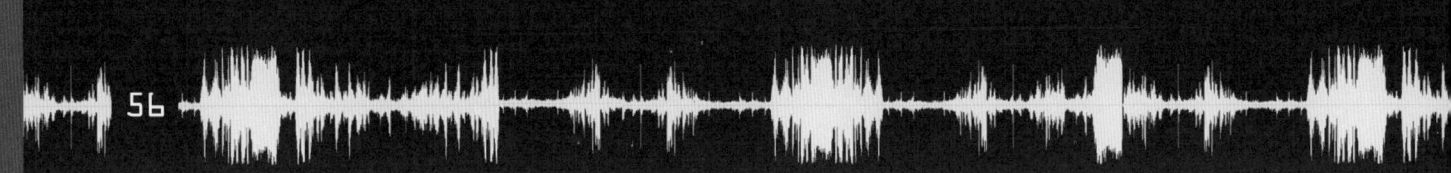

The ruins waiting to be explored.

This site has a remarkable amount of military history attached to it. The site goes back to the Revolutionary War and has been updated throughout the years as a military site. In the back, just beyond the tower, there are the remains of the original Fort that stood in Revolutionary times. There is even a small museum that is dedicated to the artillery and other weapons used throughout its history. Once upon a time, there were five massive cannons that were chained down to equally massive steel rings so that the cannons would not be ripped from their footings. These cannons fortunately never had to be fired at enemy ships entering the bay which was their main purpose.

The view from this vantage point is very beautiful as it overlooks the bay. There is a graveyard at the foot of the site which makes for double duty when investigating this area.

I had been to this location several times and have always found it interesting. The collection of EVPs never let me down, either. Every time I go there I manage to get several unexplained voices. The trick is to visit when there is no one else around since this is a public place and human contamination hinders EVP collection. I had been to Forte Revere

Mike Markowicz, Anne Kerrigan, and Ron Kolek.

Fort Revere

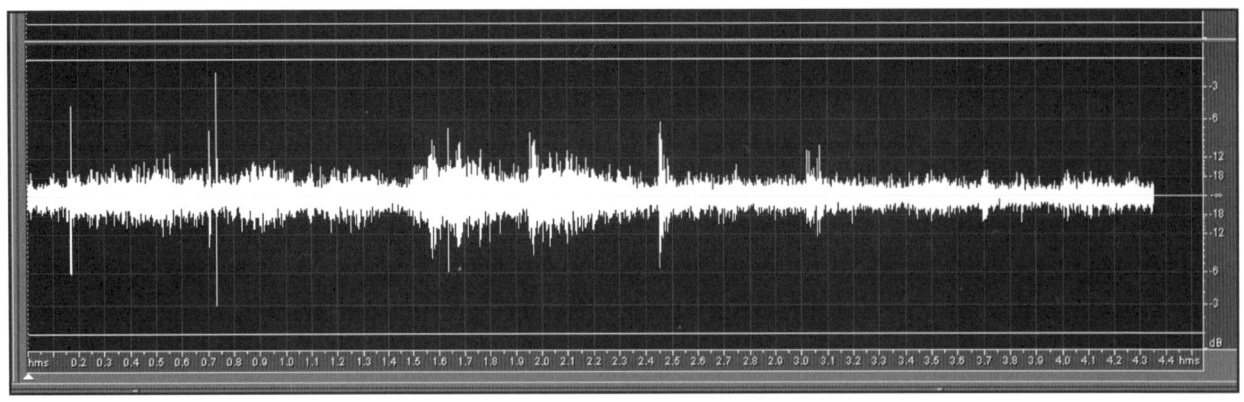

TRACK 37: **Notice the increase in decibels as the spirit says "watch you."**

with the B.O.O.O. club and have captured many great EVPs on my handheld recorder.

This first one is reminiscent of days gone by in that what the voice is saying is a term used many years ago and not much today.

This EVP is of a man saying,

"Duck shoot"

which makes sense if you are high up on a hill and have several huge cannons ready to fire at any passing ship in the bay. It would really be a duck shoot.

[Play track 36]

I believe this term means an easy shot like at a carnival when you shoot a cork gun at a target that looks like a duck.

This next clip sounds more like a female, but that can be left up to interpretation. From what I can tell, it is saying,

"Watch us watch you."

Almost to say to us that as we are watching them, they are watching us as well.

[Play track 37]

Voices can appear out of no where and come in very fast.

The voice in this clip is loud enough so that it stood out when I listened to the recordings collected from the site. Why is it so fast? It has two syllables that are spoken in less than one second. He must have been in a hurry. I can't quite make out what he is saying, but a guess is,

"no hope"

or maybe,

"go home."

[Play track 38]

Sometimes you hear something that doesn't quite sound human but are we always to assume that they will? Here is a file that fits that scenario. At first it sounds like it may be a dog barking, but we never saw a dog, nor did anyone hear one bark. It would have been noted that there was an animal if anyone saw one and this includes *any* animal because they can hinder recording whether video or audio.

To me it has three syllables and sounds like it is saying,

"terrible."

[Play track 39]

If you have audio editing software, then you can apply noise reduction and maybe slow this one down to clarify what is being said.

Ron Kolek from Ghost Chronicles joined us when we filmed the episode from this site for EBMH (*East Bridgewater's Most Haunted*). It's good to have guests when investigating sites this large because you can cover more ground. He said a shadow moved by the small window and when he went in to see if there was anyone there, no one was found. Nobody could have gotten by him without being seen. This is the kind of place where, if conditions are right, you can almost hear the spirit chattering just with your ears. I plan on going back there soon.

Spirits have control over acoustic energy. They can manipulate and transform it according to their desires.

Audio anomalies can be artifacts of EVP communication. Listen for robotic sounds, rhythmic tapping, and voice alterations when going over your evidence.

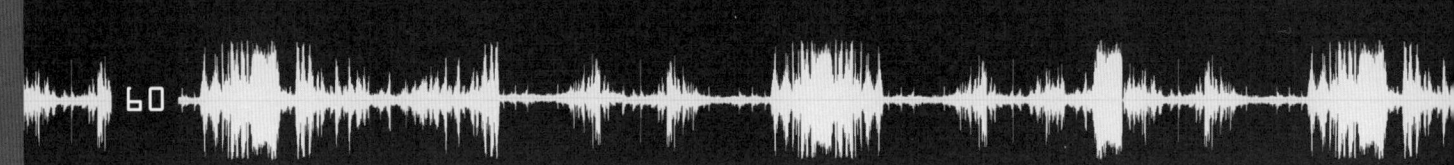

8

Palmer River Rehoboth

The old colonial graves of Palmer River.

Unmarked field stones of long forgotten citizens.

To me, an old graveyard is the perfect place to spend a sunny afternoon with a digital recorder. This was one such day.

Early in the 1700s, descendants of the first settlers of Rehoboth had spread out from the center of town, now Rumford, Rhode Island, as far east as the Palmer River.

In 1711, the Palmer River people found it too difficult to travel and attend worship at the Newman Church that was just too far away. So they partitioned the General Court in Boston to have the town divided into two separate precincts. In 1717, with the consent of the court, they began construction of a meeting house in their own part of town. The Newman

Church being the parent, had donated fifty pounds for the new construction.

The church was organized in 1721 and consisted of ten families with the Reverend David Turner as the pastor. Then on March 8, 1773, the church members voted that the meeting house be torn down and a new one built near Redway Plain, at the present site of the village cemetery. There is a sign that was erected to mark the site as a local historical landmark directly in front of the site. That makes it easier to find when driving around the small country town.

The first thing you may notice about the site is that it is just a cemetery, a very old cemetery. The earliest marked graves date back to 1675, and older still, are the markers that are only field stones, which there are many for this old cemetery. The latest marker on record dates to 1848 where Royal Ingalls was laid to rest. It was common back then just to place a stone on the gravesite of the deceased and wasn't until later that stone masons were hired to carve out what we now have as gravestones. Back then, too, there were footstones to give the orientation of the person underground.

When I investigated this site, it wasn't because the location had a major influence on the town, or had a deviant history, or that it was haunted. It was chosen by a member of B.O.O.O. because of its history alone. When you think back to the early days when the United States had not yet won its independence, our forefathers were here trying to survive.

For a hundred years prior to the Declaration of Independence being signed, people were living and dying in ordinary fashion. I do not belittle the people who are buried there, but recognize them as who they were. The farmers, blacksmiths, cobblers, and priests were bound by community that laid the way to form towns. Those towns that they developed are now our back yards.

This is an old graveyard with some markers that consist of just field stones. As you walk in, just to the left, you will find these markers. There must not have been a stone mason in town yet or they could not afford one. This was a common occurrence back then, which is why the stones were used. A large stone signified the head, a small stone the feet.

The encroaching neighborhood is evident as a new home was built just outside the property and looks out of place because of its proximity. Nevertheless it is a nice place to capture EVPs.

As I walk through the cemetery, I captured this recording of a woman softly saying,

"You won't let me know my love."

This is a good example of the sing-song fashion of speaking. The "you won't" is spoken, and the "know my love" is sung.

[Play track 40]

Rehoboth has many small cemeteries and is worth checking out. The local library may have maps of the area showing just where they are located. You may want to obtain a map because the lay of the land is a rural one, and becoming lost is easy.

The quieter the recording system, the clearer the EVPs will be.

Listening to higher frequencies can reveal excellent results with practice.

White noise works, but so does silence.

9

Guthrie Residence
East Bridgewater

**232 North Central Street
East Bridgewater, MA 02333**

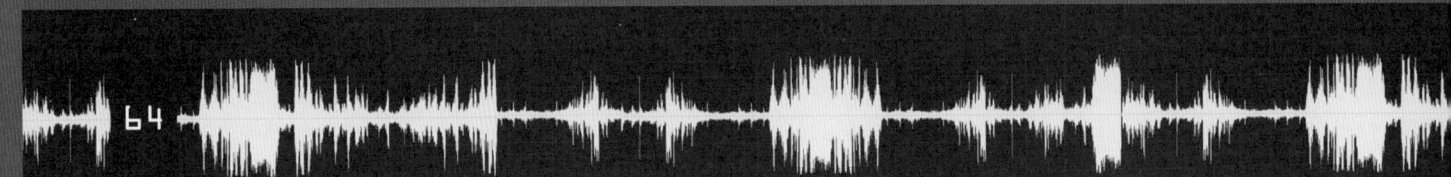

The haunted Guthrie residence.

This house was built in the 1780s by the Keith family. The exact date would need tenuous research to confirm. The house has gone through extensive rebuilding over the years, so much so that the posting of the homes "historical" placard had to be removed.

My first introduction to this house and the Guthrie family, who has currently lived there for six years, was for a preliminary investigation for a popular ghost hunting TV program. I was asked to provide the audio recordings for this investigation.

Upon entering the home, you notice the interior still has some of that old world charm of a nineteenth-century cape. The doorbell in the front hall consists of several bells that were rung by pulling a small cable. You don't see that in too many old houses nowadays. Another observance was that of a very large boulder in the basement. It must have weighed too much to remove from the site, so they built the house around it. It still has the dirt floor as it did back in the day as well, giving it much more of an ancient feeling.

The only death that can be accounted for was that of a baby who died from SIDS, however, back in the day, most people went home when they became deathly ill if they couldn't make it to a hospital. In fact, this property was actually a home clinic owned previously by a Doctor Dunn who ran his own practice from the home. And oddly enough Anne Kerrigan, who produces *East Bridgewater's Most Haunted* (EBMH), went there in her younger days for regular appointments.

The cooperation of the entire Guthrie family allowed us to investigate the home fully. The EVP results that were pulled out of that house were excellent—so much so that I wanted to put together a show for *East Bridgewater's Most Haunted* in addition to a possible mainstream program. Bob Guthrie, the homeowner, agreed to both, and so off we went recording and recording.

The interviews of the family revealed that most everyone had similar paranormal experiences. The smell of roses or perfume upstairs had been noticed by several of the family members. They heard footsteps walking upstairs. Downstairs, the bathroom door was flung open, then a bedroom door, then the front door, and finally the back door—all flew open one after the other in rapid succession! They also reported the beds shaking and vibrating, even the sensation of someone sitting on the end of the bed—disturbing to say the least. The youngest daughter experienced the suffocating weight of someone pressing her into the bed and she was helpless to stop it or cry out for help. Often though, it was just the bed shaking. Then there were the voices that accompanied her sleepless nights.

This next recording was during the interview process of the youngest daughter, now twenty-one years old.

Guthrie Residence

The interviewer was about to ask the question of how long did she live in the house and said "Okay."

An EVP then says,

"I see the pig."

[Play track 41]

The home had undergone a restoration on the back side in which the tin roof was replaced. This fact has nothing to do with the conversation during this next recording.

Sarah sitting on the bed during filming of East Bridgewater's Most Haunted.

The person being interviewed was explaining the light being turned off by itself. At the very end of the clip you can hear,

"tin roof"

spoken by a spirit.

[Play track 42]

The next recording is also from the interview process and while being asked if she feels comfortable in the home? She responds,

"Yes."

An EVP then says,

"Tattoo."

[Play track 43]

It should be noted here that the family has many tattoos and are avid automotive enthusiasts. This clip is also questionable and is left up to debate on whether it is an EVP or not. Anne Kerrigan believes this is someone sneezing which may be, however, the end result of the noise in the recorder clearly states tattoo to my ear. Again, it's left up to interpretation.

The interviewer was telling a story about how a squirrel got into his kitchen, rummaging through his counters. This can lead to strange noises if it happens at night.

At the end of the story, a childlike voice says,

"Tommy."

And another voice appears to say

"Forget."

[Play track 44]

While interviewing the son of Bob Guthrie, this voice was caught during a small break in the conversation. It says,

"Could be Esther's."

Esther is the name of Bob Guthrie's mother whom has passed over.

[Play track 45]

This clip was recorded with a handheld digital recorder and the inherent noise is obvious. The clip is in it's original recorded condition followed by a cleaned up version with noise reduction.

It appears to be a male voice saying,

"Sweets."

[Play track 46]

[Play clean track 47]

I asked the question,

"Is there anybody here with us right now?"

A long drawn out whisper then says,

"Can't ...you...see...me?"

Then another more easily heard voice says,

"You are unbelievable."

[Play track 48]

The cleaned up version has the lower frequencies cut for clarity.

[Play clean track 49]

You need to listen carefully to this one as the voices are low in volume and there is a good amount of hiss in this recording.

This next recording is rather noisy but you can make out strange-sounding voices in it.

It appears to be in the sing-song fashion and sounds like a young boy saying,

"Do you love me?"

And there is a male voice saying,

"He... won't"

afterwards.

[Play track 50]

The next clip is the cleaned up version with the lower frequencies removed for clarity.

[Play clean track 51]

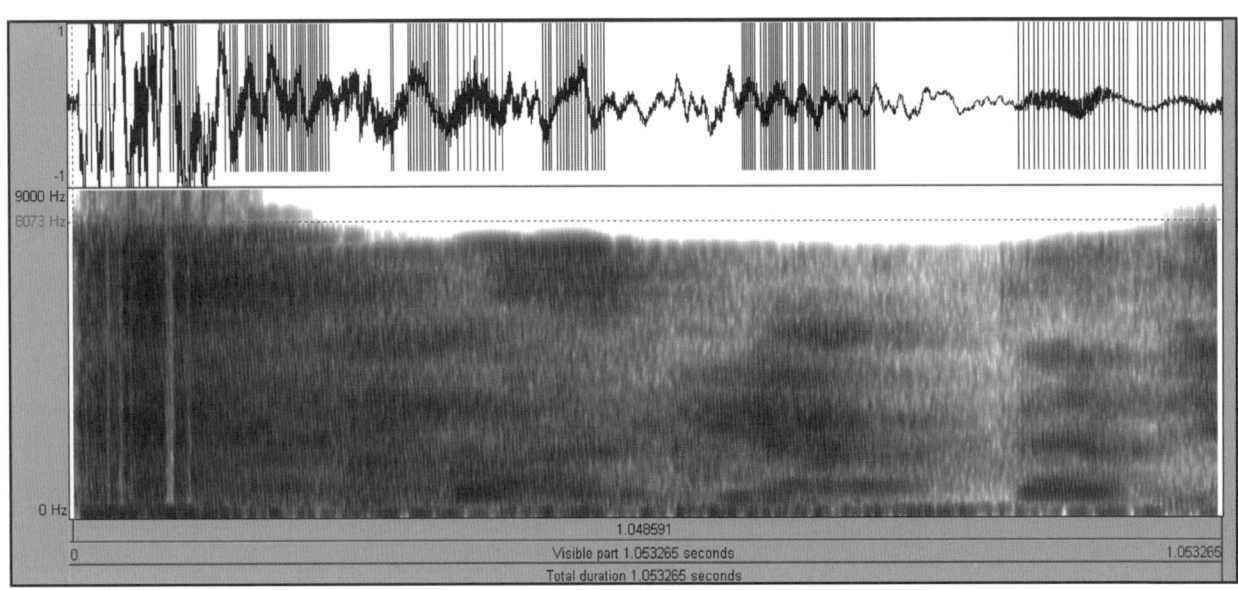

TRACK 53: The Screen Print from the PRATT voice program clearly shows the strength of the gunshot as dark shadows on the lower half of this screenshot. Also note the range and frequency spikes above all other noise that was recorded at that time.

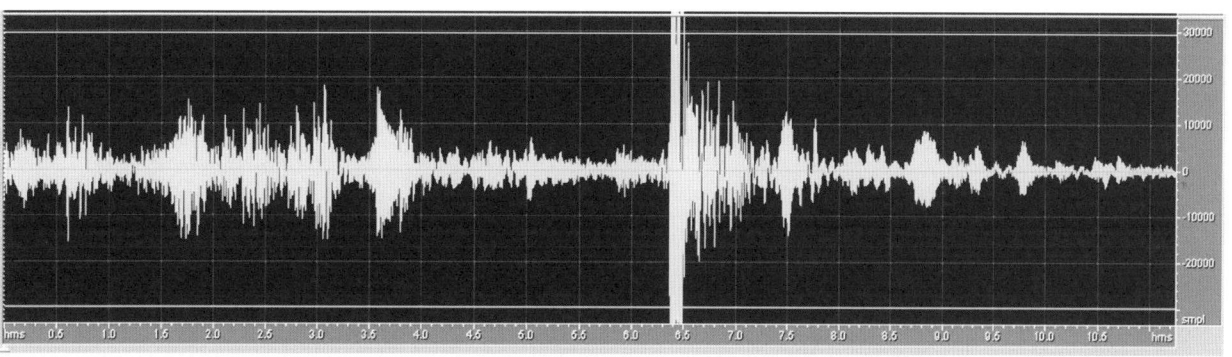

The unheard gun shot ringing out at the Guthrie residence.

This next clip is truly amazing! This is the actual recording in its original state.

I asked the question,

"Who was it that was shaking the beds trying to get someone's attention?"

A male EVP responds,

`"I hate the children."`

[Play track 52]

The voice sounds like a man in his fifties possibly and this is a fine example of a question being answered. And it may not be. Listen to it again but instead of listening to,

`"I hate the children,"`

listen for

`"I ate earlier."`

You can make out each, which is unusual but that's the way EVPs are.

This is another remarkable recording and I can offer no explanation for it. We were done recording for the evening and the family was entering back into the house.

As they did, Anne Kerrigan was explaining the smell of roses upstairs in the hallway. Then something loud is heard.

[Play track 53]

Does this sound like a gun shot? Many people believe so. If you notice right after the shot no one reacts to the sound and everyone keeps talking. A sound that loud would surely be brought to someone's attention but it just isn't heard by anyone in the room at the time!

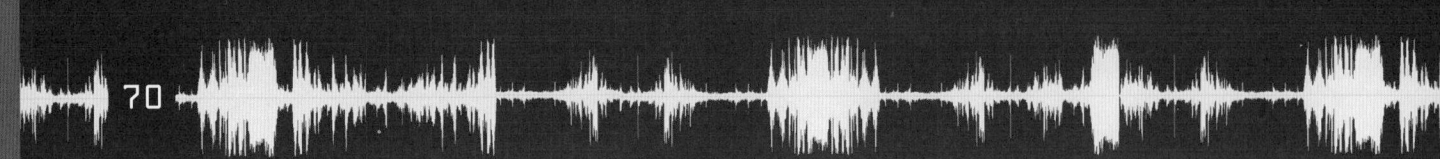

10

A Private Business Brockton

Sometimes the owners of a business or a residence may not wish to have their name or company known to the public when performing a paranormal investigation. This is one such case. So I will respect their wishes and keep their information private.

This investigation was made possible because a member of *East Bridgewater's Most Haunted,* Tom Kerrigan, worked there many years ago and was still friends of the owners and thought that this may make a good program. Although the history behind this building isn't very controversial or blood soaked, we felt because of its location being so close to a graveyard, it might reveal some good results.

The house is built close upon the boundary for a cemetery which dates from 1768. It is possibly named after a Revolutionary War Captain who lived in the local area. The home was built in 1906 by William W. Simmons who was a bricklayer. He lives there with his wife, Hattie, and their two daughters, Miriam and Blanche. It has been said that he molded the blocks for the foundation of the house with his own hands. William and Hattie lived in the house from the time it was built in 1906, until approximately 1939. Daughter Blanche married in the early 1920s and moved away. Miriam remained with her parents and never married. William died in approximately 1942. Hattie and Mariam are the only ones listed for the residence of the house until 1947, when Hattie passed away. According to city directories, Miriam and then rented out rooms in the house to other women. At some point in time, Blanche moved back into the house to live with her sister and she became the sole owner of the property when Miriam passed away in 1982. Blanche sold the house to the current owner, and no one has used the home as a residence since that time.

Just a note on how important the history is to a location: If you collect

Quite a view from a bedroom window!

any evidence, say in the form of EVPs, it will help your case by doing research for the location's previous owners and/or inhabitants. So I say thank you to Anne Kerrigan for diving into the records at all the Town halls along the way. Anne provided the program and the investigators with valuable information.

It is an eerie feeling to look out your bedroom window and see a grave yard just feet from your home. I can only imagine what it must have been like for a child to experience this feeling while looking out those windows. And what would their friends say? I wonder if they had Halloween parties and found their way into the graveyard at midnight for a treat.

Two investigations were done in this building—one with B.O.O.O. and the

A Private Business

other with the *East Bridgewater's Most Haunted* team.

First and foremost, this building was a home, and only as of late has it been converted into a business so the place still has a home feel to it.

Upon entering, one does not get the impression that the place is alive with spirits, however, there were many EVPs that were collected. It has a wonderful staircase that leads to the second floor as well as an interesting floor layout. Up in the attic, two sensitive people, one on each of the two investigations, felt that there were children playing and hiding in a specific section just under the rafters. Maybe they were playing hide and seek?

During the initial walkthrough, Tom pointed out the offices upstairs. He had several experiences on the second floor and was going over what he had felt. One such experience was feeling a cold breeze that moved a closed door back and forth, even though there was no air conditioning in the room. He continued telling us about the offices, and the following clip shows that spirits do indeed have a sense of humor.

Tom says,

"In here, was one of our..."

An EVP says,

`"And he doesn't see the light."`

Tom says,

"...In here, was one of our, ah, offices for somebody that was..."

[Play track 54]

Tom can be heard trying to turn on the light to show us the office, but the light was not working. You can hear the switch being turned on and off several times in vain. Later, Tom tried the light again and it worked perfectly! Play this file again now that you know the scenario and you can see the humor this spirit has.

There is a staircase just off of the living room that has a nice look and feel to it where we filmed the opening and closing sequences to EBMH as I sat on one of the bottom steps.

Hoping to catch the spirit of a child, I said,

"You shouldn't play on the stairs."

A loud whispery voice almost yells out,

`"Why not?"`

[Play track 55]

This is a nice loud voice even though it appears to be whispering. Why not speak with a more human sounding voice? Why whisper? These questions we just do not have answers for. One reason may be one of energy, going back to my theory that the more strong your mind is, the louder the voice may be when it crosses over into our world from theirs. Maybe the conditions were exact and this is all that could make it through? This kind of voice is very prominent and makes up most of what I have recorded.

Stairs are always a focal point in a house, just like a kitchen. Stairs are used all the time and care must be used when traveling up and down them. Children and adults fall down them, sometimes getting injured. The same is true for walking up them and tripping, only to fall down. As a kid, I fell while going up the stairs because I was running. When my father found I was okay he made me walk up and down the stairs ten times to teach me a lesson so I would not be hurt in the future. It is always a good idea to spend time investigating a staircase if the house has one. Ask questions about children and safety.

In this clip I say,

"Shall we upstairs?"

Tom says,

"Sure."

Then an EVP of what sounds like an elderly woman says,

```
"Stay off the stairs,
        Michael."
```

[Play track 56]

What a creepy sounding voice!

This clip comes from the evening when B.O.O.O. came along to lend a hand in the investigation. Once everyone was safely upstairs with no injuries, we proceeded to ask questions and record the general conversations about the house. This file is an eye opener and gives insight to the abilities of the spirits.

One of members, Patrick could not make it that night and it appears the spirit knew it.

The voice says,

```
"Where is Patrick?"
```

The word "where" is spoken normally, but the word "is" is spoken in a very low voice, and "Patrick" is spoken normally.

[Play track 57]

Why the drop in frequency? Is it necessary or is that just a normal occurrence when spirits speak to us? Conditions that we don't fully understand certainly must be at play. This passage shows the awareness of the spirit because he knew who Patrick was and has the awareness that he isn't coming to the investigation as he asks where Patrick is.

At one point, I took a condenser microphone with me upstairs to the attic to see what I could pick up. I shut off all the mics and we headed up. Little did I

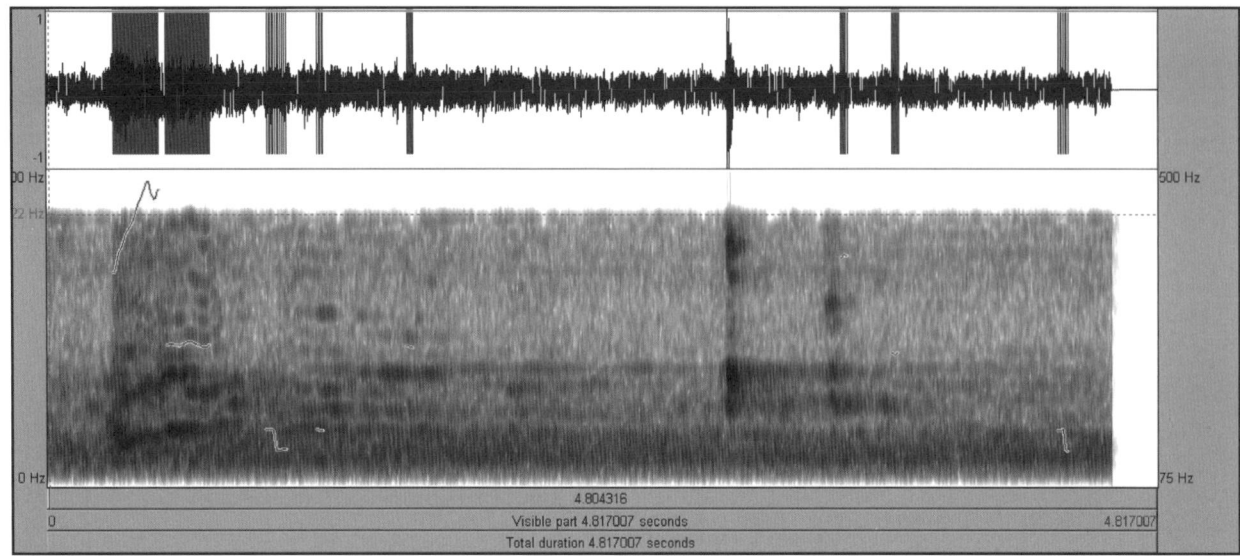

TRACK 58: The small lines that are drawn on the bottom half of this screen print shows the pitch within the associated frequencies from the child-like singing. You will notice the first one on the left rises and then drops slightly and is somewhat broken up. The background is also darkened showing strength in decibels. The next noticeable characteristic is the darkened area showing strength in decibels again as the man says, "tch, it's okay" and also shows pitch. The vertical lines that appear on the top portion of this screenshot show pulses that are attributable to human voices.

know at the time that I had inadvertently shut off the mic I was holding and left a mic on downstairs. What was recorded was the room with no one in it, no activity. We could not even be heard two floors up but something strange came through. I cannot explain the odd sounding voices in this next clip as no one was there and the doors were all locked.

> It starts with what appears to be a child saying something unknown. A voice follows apparently answering the child with,
>
> "Tch it's okay."
>
> This is the original recorded track and it has not been altered.

The reverb from the voice of the man is what came through when he spoke.

[Play track 58]

If you look at the dynamic of the situation, a child is making a statement and an older man is telling him it is okay, comforting him. Has he been charged with looking after the young boy? It has been said that there is work in the afterlife, and maybe this is a glimpse into just what kind of work there is. Looking after troubled ones that need direction much like the way it is now for us.

Another phenomenon in regards to the way voices may sound can be found in this next clip. Sometimes a musicality is associated when a voice comes in. This one was recorded in the attic and is very musical. Why this is so is unknown for sure.

The voice appears to sing,

"He comes."

[Play track 59]

It almost sounds like a musical instrument.

Sometimes, a voice tells a story that may not be known otherwise. It never shows up in any form of history so we take it for what it is, a story, more accurately a statement. This clip is one of those, but it has a name that may be factual. We just don't know at this time. More research into the name needs to be given to check it out.

The voice is again in the loud whispery style saying,

"Governor Lincoln's head blew off today."

[Play track 60]

Was Abraham Lincoln ever a Governor? I know a cemetery in Hingham that has his descendants buried there. Maybe one of them is who the voice is talking about? Just how factual is what he is saying? I would have to assume that if a descendent of Abraham Lincoln met the same fate as getting shot in the head, it would make news all across the United States and abroad.

This investigation spanned two nights and a day and yielded many great EVPs. We even caught one faint orb of light floating by the infrared camera. The house has a vibe to it but is homey enough. Please note that the building is off limits and has a security system in place to deter anyone from entering the building.

To contact
East Bridgewater's Most Haunted,
email them at:
ebmosthaunted@yahoo.com

11

William L. White Mansion Taunton

The Beautiful White's Mansion

242 Winthrop Street
Taunton, MA 02718

This beautiful home was built in 1873 and is one of the largest and more elaborate Mansard style homes in Taunton. It has a belcast Mansard roof that still has the patterned slates. It also has a Palladian type window and authentic Tiffany stained glass on its stair case landing. This house was built for William L. White Sr., but he could only enjoy it for two years because he passed away. However, he did pass it onto his son, William L. White Jr. The home served as a local landmark for many years and was part of the "Whites' Four Corners" which is located at the intersection of Winthrop and Highland Streets. Business must have been doing well because the Whites also owned three other homes on those corners. Sadly though, only the one standing today has survived.

William White Sr. had a carriage manufacturing company named Peck and White where they made horse-drawn carriages. He was a prominent businessman in Taunton at the time and ran the business. Peck and White was located at 21-29 Weir Street in the late 1800s just off of the Taunton Green and unfortunately has succored to time and no longer remains.

During the investigation of the third floor in between the living room and the adjacent room, there is a decorative structure reminiscent of an old-fashioned pocket door. It is the kind that slips into the wall. (It looks like that and may have

The beautiful White's mansion.

been, but I don't know for sure.) The top of this structure is boarded off; however, if you lift off the one board that is loose, you can see the remnants of a couple of interesting things.

First, there is the evidence of a fire that can be seen as soot. In 1910, there was indeed a fire in the front of the house. It is very interesting to see something tragically historical about a house like that, soot from a fire almost 100 years ago that almost destroyed the remaining mansion of the White family. You can reach up and touch it! Also in

William L. White Mansion

The original Tiffany stained glass window.

that small space is a small fragment of old wallpaper. Its red and gold colors remind you of just what it must have looked like back in the day. It must have been a very rich looking home, and rightfully so.

I had investigated this home on three occasions and came away with some very good EVPs, some of which were surprising. Investigations included Elizabeth Russell who was a tenant on the second floor and lived there for six years. During that time, she told me that there were many accounts of paranormal activity going on. There were the reports of someone walking down the hall with heavy feet in the third floor apartment even though it was empty. Even someone running down the hall like a child was witnessed by Elizabeth. She told me

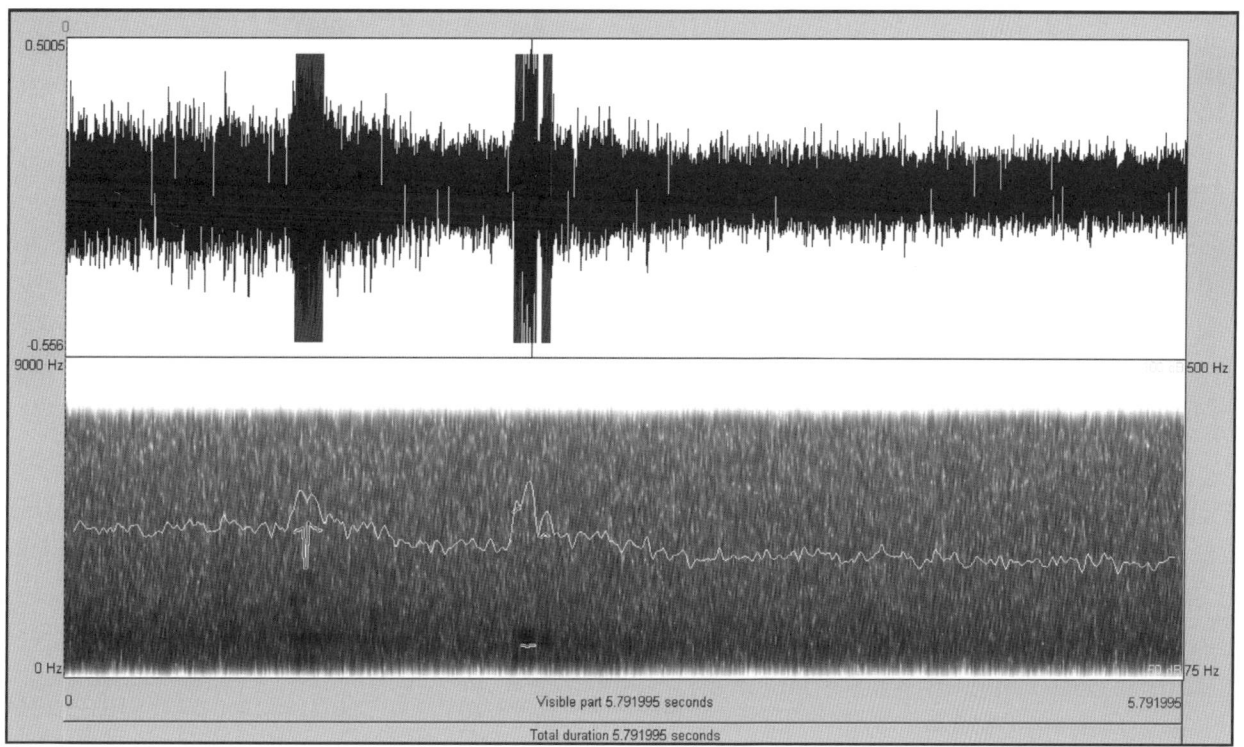

TRACK 61: The squiggly line that is seen drawn across the bottom of the screen shot denotes intensity of decibels as well as the darkened back ground showing decibel strength. There is also a small amount of pitch shown and is represented by the small lines underneath the continuous "intensity" line. The top half of the screen shot shows the decibels increase when the girl says, "spanked" and "wrongly," and appear as a rise in decibels which is the broadest range of spikes shown.

of the time when she was sitting in her living room when, all of the sudden, at ten o'clock, a loud thud was heard like someone dropped a washing machine on the floor above. And it happened more than once! She was shaken by this account and had no explanation for it. The house was as solid as the day it was made.

One night when Elizabeth was about to go to sleep, she felt as if someone was spooning up behind her. Her back felt tingly and warm as if someone was encroaching upon her. This kind of account can only be truly realized by the participant.

When it was time for Elizabeth to leave her apartment, she was packing up her belongings when she noticed a sterling silver bracelet just in front of the closet doorway. It did not belong to her and she had never seen it before during the six years she'd stayed at the house. It clearly looked to be old, but she had no explanation as to why it was there or who it belonged to.

William L. White Mansion

This EVP was recorded on the third floor. Oddly enough, the microphone that was turned on was located in the living room, and the microphone that I thought was on, was not. We were asking questions in the small room next to the living room with the mic off, unbeknownst to me until afterwards.

This recording is that of a young girl with an English or Irish accent and has a good deal of reverb to it. She appears to be saying,

```
"I spanked them wrongly,
      yes sir"
```

as if she was being asked why she had hit someone.

[Play track 61]

That must mean she had spanked more than one person. Can this mean that she is looking after some children and they were spanked by this person with this young voice? Then they told on her or got caught doing so? We will never know.

This next clip was taken from the second floor apartment. The voice was found in the silence in between questioning and had nothing to do with it.

It is of a man saying,

```
"The Devil, never appears."
```

You will hear the heating system popping as the apartment has been fitted with new baseboard heat.

[Play track 62]

This clip was recorded in the back yard right in front of the steel bulkhead door. It was recorded with a Sony handheld digital recorder.

You can hear this child's voice in a somewhat sing-song fashion say,

```
"I love you Daddy."
```

[Play track 63]

It is high in frequency and can easily be heard. Also there is a note of the time it was recorded— 2am. There were no children around outside at that time of night. We never heard or saw any one.

I have been to the White's Mansion several times with different groups of people, including an area paranormal group. Each time I go there and record, I capture EVPs. The large house is an active one and I don't think there is anything malevolent that resides there. There was a lot of living that went on here and I believe that all the recordings point in the same direction. That is to say, the house, for the most part, has everyday living contained within the many voices I have recorded.

12

McArdell Residence
Plymouth

McArdell Residence.

McArdell Residence

Cindy McArdell, had contacted me about performing a paranormal investigation in her house because she had experienced a lot of unexplainable activity. She also agreed to let us film for the local cable show, *East Bridgewater's Most Haunted*.

The accounts told to me by Cindy include footsteps being heard in the upstairs hall when no one was there, human-looking faces being seen in a floor standing mirror and full-bodied apparitions of three different spirits have been seen by her family members. Shadow people walk the hall upstairs and the house cat sees these spirits and watches them as they move about. A small boy was seen by Cindy running up the stairs, and upon searching for him, no one was found in the entire house. Many babysitters refused to return over the years because of the feelings of being watched as well as their own feelings about the house being haunted. There has been the smell of pipe smoke in the basement, high orb activity in photographs when shooting the dining room, and swings outside swinging by themselves, with only one swinging at a time, not affected by the wind as a whole. A roll of paper towels unraveled itself at a high rate of speed and spilled onto the kitchen floor as witnessed by Cindy and her children.

The accounts of activity go on and on, and it sounded too good to be true! The latest was an audible sound of glass breaking in Cindy's bedroom. She immediately searched the entire room looking for the glass but she did not find anything. No broken glass. This is the kind of thing that happens to you and you can't explain it or show people the evidence. But you know what you've heard or seen.

It has been said that everyone who has been in the house has come away with an experience of their own. This led me to investigate these accounts and Cindy agreed to allow us to film there for the show thankfully. We had a full crew that day including my wife, Paula, who used a handheld recorder. We had the infrared cameras hooked up to a DVR, a nice studio quality Sony camera on tripod, my recording system and handheld video and audio recorders. Anne Kerrigan uses a pendulum for questions and answers part of the show. An EMF (Electro Magnetic Field) meter was also used to measure any fluctuations in the surrounding fields.

Cindy had always had the impression that anything in the house was not there to harm her or her family. She feels that the house is like Grand Central Station with its own fair share of paranormal activity coming and going through out the house. After examining the audio files, I have to agree with Cindy. There were many low volume voices to be heard with only a couple of louder ones

The hallway where black figures roam.

that were more easily understood. When I played the files for her, she was relieved that it appeared her thoughts about the house were correct. There were several clips of bad language, although nothing serious. Mostly, there were whispering and non confrontational speech patterns. If any spirit was aiming to get through to Cindy, they would do so in a more strong fashion with a louder voice. The strength I believe has a lot to do with the intent of the spirit. Whispering between themselves and swearing at Cindy are two different scenarios.

This clip is that of a woman saying,

```
"You bastard,"
```

and a male EVP saying,

```
"Bullsh--."
```

It is followed by a woman saying,

```
"Your friend Arrow bet me."
```

[Play track 64]

First of all, it is not clear if she means me or Tom Kerrigan, our camera man for

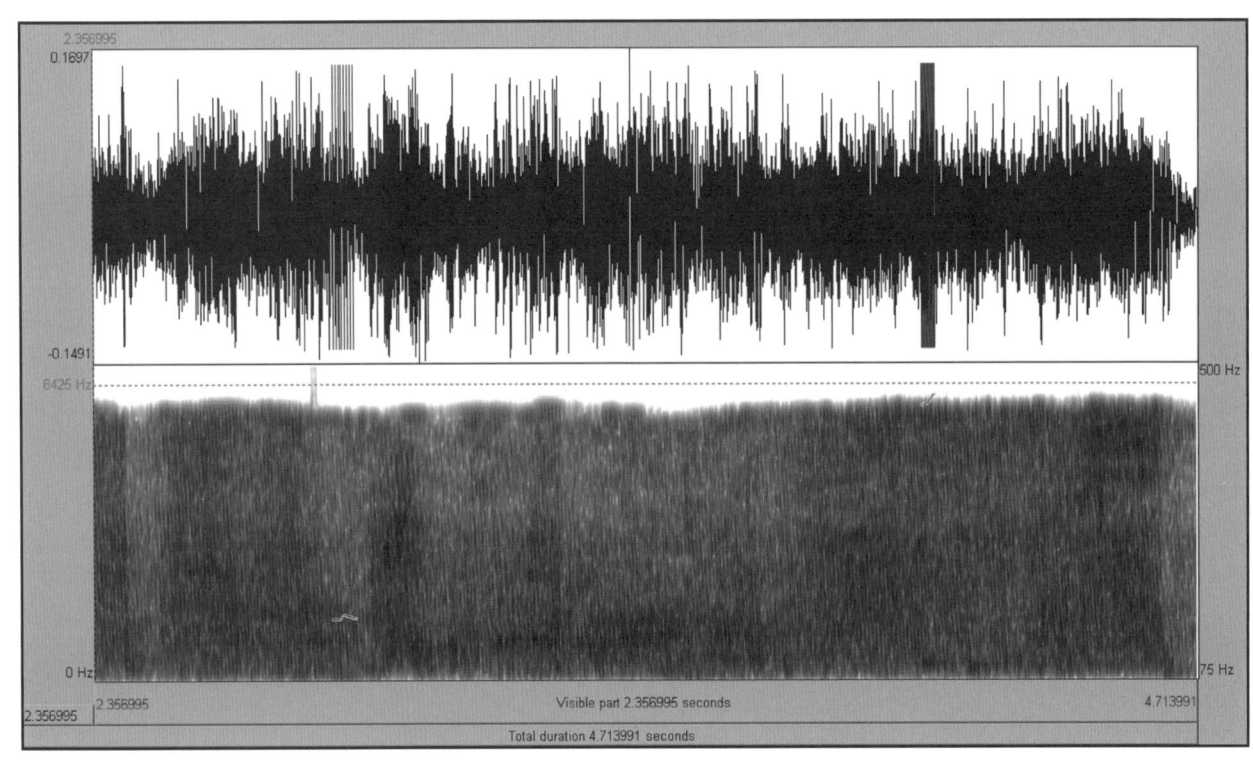

TRACK 65: This is a picture of Cool Edit's spectral image of the audio file. The whiter the areas are within that frequency, the stronger its decibel signature is. The word "astrograph" appears strong under 1000 Hz and the word "please" can be seen on the far right of the screen and spikes above 7500 Hz. Its brightness shows the strength of the voice as it speaks into the room in which it was recorded.

this investigation. It also sounds like there are two voices here, one whispery and the other, a younger voice. Both are saying the same thing. Obviously someone is disagreeing with her and responds with a swear word. There is a woman's laugh right before the woman says, "your friend" and this is one of the investigators down stairs at the control point where all the recording equipment is.

And that brings up a good point. The direction of a response may or not be aimed towards the one asking questions. If the spirits are arguing and only one small piece of the conversation comes through, then does that mean that maybe a "shut up" was directed at you? It has to be relative to someone but we just cannot tell for sure.

When Ann and I were upstairs in the front bedroom, the rest of the crew was downstairs in the dining room at the control point. We asked the usual questions like, is anyone here and do you have anything to say? These are standard, but it is also helpful just to talk among yourselves about the way the area feels and the impressions you are getting. Talk about some history or say the names of people who were known to live in the house. I was commenting on how I hadn't gotten the heebie jeebies from the room we were in and Anne hadn't either. Then an apparent man's voice is heard. I am not sure what he is saying and I get conflicting results when trying to figure it out.

[Play track 65]

For a reference I hear,

`"Astrograph."`

People hear different things when playing this file and that is just another amazing thing about EVPs.

This house has a nice old-world charm to it and feels warm and cozy. I never felt the presence of bad spirits nor has Cindy reported any. The shadow people that move through the house, primarily on the second floor, have no interaction with anyone who lives there. They just seem to be passing through—just like most of the activity from the other spirits.

Cindy has reported that there are times when the activity heightens, like when the seasons change; then things start happening around the house. Items are moved or knocked over and the footsteps appear out of thin air. The audio recordings brought to light that there is a lot of chatter here, but low in volume. Spirits seem to be going about their business, not bothering anyone. A busy train station, indeed.

Sometimes it works out that when the owner feels something to be true about their house, paranormally speaking, that the collected evidence points in the same direction. The McArdell residence is one such place.

My thanks go out to Cindy and her family for allowing EBMH into her home for a great experience.

13

The Town Hall
East Bridgewater

The old Hobart Estate now the East Bridgewater Town Hall and Police Department.

The Town Hall

This was my first time investigating in front of a video camera for a show on the paranormal. We filmed the Town Hall for our local cable station for *East Bridgewater's Most Haunted* on September 15, 2006. The scenario was to go into a location said to be haunted, film and record audio, and build a show from that data. If we can take a step back one year earlier, it was my intent to produce such a program. After taking the course at the cable station located in the high school, though, I found time for such a program almost impossible to handle. Enter Ann Kerrigan, now the producer of EBMH. She'd had the same idea as I'd had one year earlier. I saw on an email that someone was looking for help with forming a show on the paranormal so I emailed the station

Anne Kerrigan of *East Bridgewater's Most Haunted.*

my information. Russ Hannigan, the cable station director, contacted me to see if I was still interested. I was, and the rest they say is history.

Ann and I hit it off, as we both had a love for all things paranormal and creating a program surrounding it. This would turn out to be not only a lot of fun but also a good learning and networking tool. There are many paranormal groups in Massachusetts and we have had some investigate with us when filming the show. It is a great way to meet people in the field of paranormal research.

Ann talked to the town selectman to gain access to the Town Hall building at night for us to have total access to investigate. All access was granted and off we went. There were only three of us that night, Anne Kerrigan, Russ Hannigan, and myself. I was the more seasoned one of the group, so maybe that's why Anne told me to be the host while the camera was rolling. I just started speaking and luckily it turned out okay. (Even though I was chewing gum at the time!) Anne and Russ were brand new to the field, which made for an interesting night. The air conditioning was on, though, which did hinder the audio recordings somewhat.

There was nothing on video to point in the direction of anything paranormal, but the EVPs were something else. There is a water pump that is in the wall near the elevator that would periodically turn on as the water level ran low and needed filling. I thought the noise would be a real nuisance, but it turned out to be just the opposite. As we asked a question the pump turned on almost like clockwork on several questions. Almost like it was talking directly to us! Upon review of the audio files it was discovered that someone was indeed talking back! They were using the acoustic energy from the sound of that pump to communicate.

There is a tale about Mrs. Hobart being seen and her presence felt by the employees who work in this building. There is an elevator that goes down to the police station but you need a key in order to operate it. That elevator has been seen working all by itself! The doors would close and it would proceed to the first floor and the doors would open. The policeman on duty would check to see who had used the elevator but no one would be there. This has happened on several occasions. Naturally, we had to ask if it was Mrs. Hobart who was using that elevator.

If you listen carefully, you will hear a voice say,

`"Yes, I push buttons."`

[Play track 66]

Another fact about the building is that it used to have a service elevator located near the front door. Mrs. Hobart did use it to get up stairs easier in her

The Town Hall

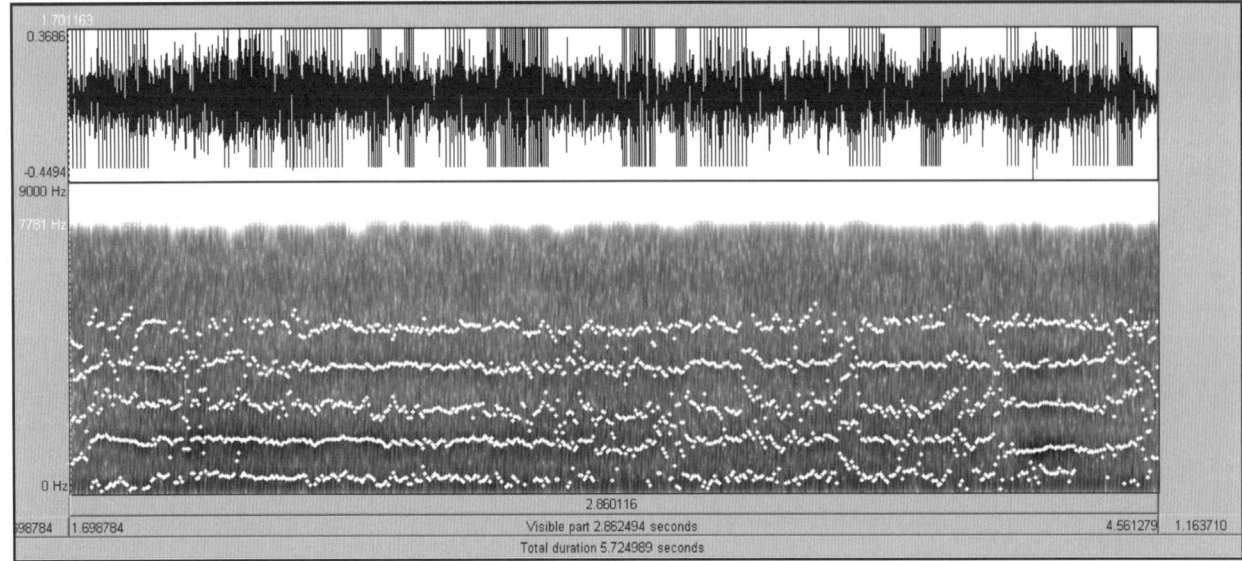

TRACK 66: This screenshot of the voice program PRATT shows strong formant formation across the sound of the pump and the EVP. There are also pulses that show on the top portion of this screenshot as straight vertical lines, however, they are broken up. Human speaking voices have a more tightly packed unit of measure regarding this kind of graph, therefore, it is inconclusive. However the voice is audible.

later years. An interesting note about this recording is, how do the spirits know exactly when the pump will turn on? The sentence starts when the pump turns on and ends when the pump turns off, with perfect timing. It is almost as if they can see the energy and use it at their will, as it appears here. There is no other way to predict exactly when it will turn on and for its duration. Unless time itself can also be manipulated, I see no other way to cause this to happen. But there it is.

This next clip has two voices speaking at the same time in sync as the pump turns on. You will have to listen carefully for each message as you play the clip. Russ Hannigan asks,

"Is there a message you'd like to pass onto someone?"

The voices reply,

`"No more questions."`

And,

`"Yes he speaks."`

[Play track 67]

Layered on top of each other, sharing the same energy wave must be just like talking over one another in this life. That is a common enough trait of speaking and maybe it is so in the spirit world as well?

The history of the Hobart Estate is interesting as Aaron Hobart had a very political life that he brought with him to East Bridgewater. Aaron Hobart was born on June 26, 1787, and was a U.S. Representative from Massachusetts. Born in Abington, Massachusetts, Hobart pursued classical studies and graduated from Brown University in 1805. He studied law, was admitted to the bar and commenced practice in Abington. He served as a member of the Massachusetts House of Representatives and served in the Massachusetts State Senate. Hobart was elected as a Democratic Republican to the 17th Congress, elected as an Adams Clay Republican to the 18th Congress, reelected as an Adams candidate to the 19th Congress, and served from November 4, 1820, to March 3, 1827.

He declined to be a candidate for renomination in 1826. He then served as an executive counselor from 1827 to 1831 and served as judge of probate from 1843 to 1858. He died in East Bridgewater Massachusetts September 19, 1858, and was buried in Central Cemetery.

The results were surprising from that evening of recording. It may have to do with the Town Hall being a home first but who really knows for sure? The evidence speaks for itself and being able to get in there on a regular basis after hours to conduct paranormal investigations to collect more is highly unlikely. So we will take it as it is, active.

> Don't be afraid to experiment with different recording techniques. They all work.
>
> Try rubbing your hands together in a circular motion after asking a question. That sound is prime for EVP collection.

14

The Inn at Washington Square Salem

53 Washington Square North
Salem, MA 01970-4020

Sometimes, when you meet people through investigating, they turn out to be good friends. This real life story is one of them. I had been on Lights Out Radio a couple of times and must have made an impression on hostess Robyne Marie because she invited me to the initial investigation of the inn.

Robyne Marie's involvement with this inn is to be the event coordinator for paranormal groups that want to collect evidence from such a place. She also is an excellent medium with a success rate in the high nineties! She is a psychologist and works with area police departments to help solve cases.

This was to be no ordinary recording session as the inn keepers want to open this charming bed and breakfast to the paranormal community. If the results of investigating were positive, then they could say, at the very least, the place yielded great results. Giving the B&B a "haunted" status would need many more recording sessions along with video and photography data to say that it is indeed haunted. As time rolls on, the collection of evidence may just bring along the title "haunted." However, I did get quite a lot of EVPs from my initial investigation. A total of seventy clips of voices were collected in one evening, starting at the front door before I even stepped foot inside! I always start my recorder before I go into the place I am to investigate.

As I entered the inn, I was greeted warmly by Robyne Marie and the owners,

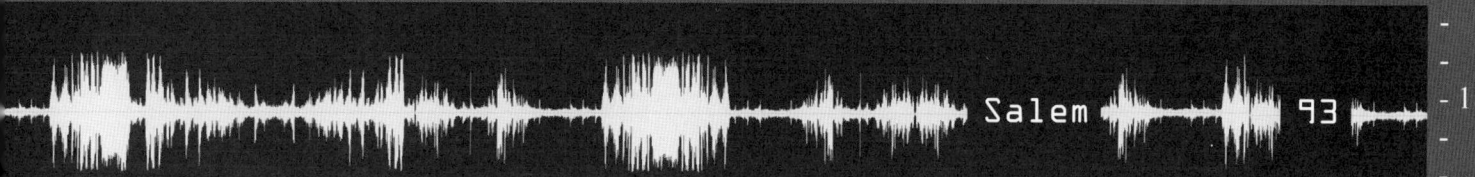

Salem's first haunted B&B open for business. *Photo courtesy of Robyne Marie.*

Bob Marcey and Paul Stream. They were anxious to see if the old Victorian-style house could yield any paranormal evidence to support the claims of it being haunted, as the owners and guest alike felt it was.

What a beautifully decorated inn! It is everything you would expect from an old Victorian house built in 1837, with lots of pictures, clocks, and furniture in all of the rooms. You get that cozy feeling when sitting on the couch in the front parlor or any one of the rooms that are for rent. There are three generations of Bobs' own family adorning the walls and display cases of personal belongings from them are located in the parlor. It is almost like a time capsule his family! And Bob knows who they are and when they lived as well. There is rich history on all floors and this sets the stage for paranormal investigating. It has the look, but does it have the goods?

When I talked to Robyne about the inn and why she thinks it is haunted, she told me she had sensed energy flowing through and around certain areas on every floor. When she was in the basement, performing a walkthrough, she had "seen a full-bodied apparition that lasted for a good twenty minutes!"

When owner, Paul, walked through the area, he got a strong chill. A very noticeable cold spot was exactly where the apparition was located! This is one of those "you had to be there" moments. If you were there and felt the coldness, would you believe it?

Paul has seen a spirit appear to him as a very tall man about six-foot-four with a top hat on and a white shirt with riding-style pants. This spirit appeared to him for about twenty-five seconds from the corner of his eye.

The belief is that this might be the funeral director who owned the house at one time. The house was not a funeral parlor, just the house in which he lived. Paul didn't want him to fade from view so he sat there without moving a muscle. When the spirit moved his hand upwards, he turned to look, and it was gone. This was the same man that Robyne has seen in the doorway of the Honeymoon Suite that is located in the back on the first floor. He was also present during my initial investigation and seen by Robyne. Perhaps this man is the caretaker of the horses that one of the owners had. She kept seeing "the horses, the horses." She asked questions about just who and what this person had to do with the horses, and she picked up that they rode them and cared for them. Since the inn was also a funeral parlor at one time, maybe this man had something to do with that line of business? In the old days, a horse-drawn hearse was what they used. We don't really know who he is at this point, but maybe further research may reveal his identity.

Robyne also has felt the presence of a beautiful elderly woman named Sarah sitting in a chair with newspapers on her lap. Newspapers kept coming in, newspapers and more newspapers. Her face was pale but very pretty for her age. "She is a very well-read lady. She likes to keep up with the news," Robyne said while I was recording. She also said that there was something about a boy—maybe a paperboy? She asked for more information from the spirit she was communicating with but didn't get much more information than that.

It was later confirmed by the next door neighbors who actually knew Sarah when she lived there. They told Robyne that she did in fact have pale skin but was a very pretty lady. When she was found in her house, she was sitting on her chair with a newspaper on her lap! There were newspapers piled up in that room where she was found. I guess you could say she was well read. The paperboy it seems liked to actually go inside her house and hand her newspaper to her directly. She must have struck up quite a friendship with him over the years of delivering the paper. Well Robyne was right on with her visions, or should I say communications!

She also has seen and felt the energy flow through this house and has seen and communicated with several of its spiritual inhabitants. This clip demonstrates her ability to hear them.

She identifies someone named Vicky.

The spirit says,

```
"Vicky, that's the one."
```

Robyne says,

"Vicky,"

immediately afterwards. Talk about being right on!

[Play track 68]

Robyne picked up on this spirit of Vicky several times during the evening and to capture an EVP saying *Vicky* is exceptional. I wasn't one for believing in what mediums say they are sensing, but Robyne has changed my mind! There are several recordings that prove the fact that she does indeed pick up on spirit activity. Several reveal direct communication between her and the spirits. She's my new BFF!

The Honeymoon Suite is very nice and has its own hot tub in the bedroom, its own bathroom and a huge bed. It keeps with the tradition of the Victorian-era décor and is quite a lovely room. This is where the man in the top hat has been seen entering and even standing in the doorway. The energy seems to flow right into that room from the dining area.

Upstairs in the front bedroom, Robyne felt that energy again flowing into the room and around the foot of the bed. She asked the presence,

"Would you like to tell us your name?"

An EVP responds with,

"I've been sitting here, don't you see me?"

Then an investigator says,

"Mary said this room was relatively quiet."

Robyne says,

"This is the only spot that I felt something before."

Again an EVP responds, but noticeably a female voice says,

"It's Robyne."

And then a male voice says,

"Like I care."

[Play track 69]

What an incredible recording! The first voice saying *I've been sitting here* as Robyne picks up on the energy is truly amazing to watch in action. This recording clearly shows her ability to pick up the energy from spirits as they communicate to us. The recording also shows an interaction between a female spirit that actually knows about Robyne, as she is happy to see her. Her male friend does not seem to share in her enthusiasm.

There are also names that have been recorded. This one is a very clear one and I believe that it is a phenomenon I like to call re-modulated acoustic sound energy. What I think happens is when a person or some other sound is produced by us, a spirit or entity remodels the sound or transforms it to sound the way they want it to. In most cases it is one of speech, as is the case with the next file.

This sounds like the voice of an investigator who was down the hall saying,

"My name's Steven Hunt. I'm a junkie cokehead, you get that?"

[Play track 70]

This is no big deal if the investigator's name was Steven Hunt, but it's not. The voice is spoken and not whispered, but it does not even raise the decibel metering on my computer screen. A human voice always does, according to proximity, because the energy will register robustly in decibels giving a clear measurement. One more point, this person and the rest of the team had no idea of the name Hunt before this investigation occurred. Hunt is the name of the family who built the house! So far, Steven Hunt has not been identified as being part of that family.

Another name that came in very clearly,

"This is Frederick Germane Pun."

[Play track 71]

The scenario is the same as with the name Steve Hunt. No registry on the decibel meter, just a nice clear voice saying a name. It also has a good amount of what sounds like a fast echo to it. Usually, it's reverb that the voices seem to have when they are this strong. It's not a rule, just an observation. You can really hear it when he says Pun and the sound trails off.

This clip is the only spirit of a child recorded at the Inn that evening. It appears to be a boy saying,

"I'm Brandon."

[Play track 72]

He speaks in a half breathy voice as if too weak to form the words any stronger. It almost seems like he wanted us to hear his voice so he speaks it when he can. Nothing more was recorded of this little voice. So sweet.

This next clip is just the sort of thing any medium would be proud to hear. It's a message of what communicating within the spirit world is all about. It has been my belief that when someone communicates with a spirit, information is passed to each other in the form of thought. This is to include emotions, smells, words and images just like a memory you might have, only this is being given to you.

In this next clip Robyne senses that there was a little girl present.

"Was that the little girl?"

An EVP says,

"Um hm."

Robyne says,

"Who's Theresa?"

Then an EVP says,

"Look through this soul and find her family."

[Play track 73]

Does this mean this person knows this little girl, and through memory contained in their soul the information can be reached somehow? What an amazing recording! It's times like these that I am forever thankful for the plentiful recordings that I continue to capture—they never cease to amaze me. This kind of recording opens up interesting conversations about how EVPs speak to one another and to us as well.

The place has its fair share of spirits speaking unkindly and using swear words. The following clip is a very interesting one and shows the battle for good and evil even on the other side.

You will hear a male voice say,

"The devil make you live long."

And over that, is another male voice whispering,

"No he won't."

[Play track 74]

This track has been amplified so the voices that were recorded low in volume can be heard well enough to make out what is being said. (I almost never use anything but amplification when preparing files.) I was also told to

F*** off

as I was coming downstairs. When Bob the owner was showing us around the basement and telling us the feelings he has for the space, a voice chimes in and says,

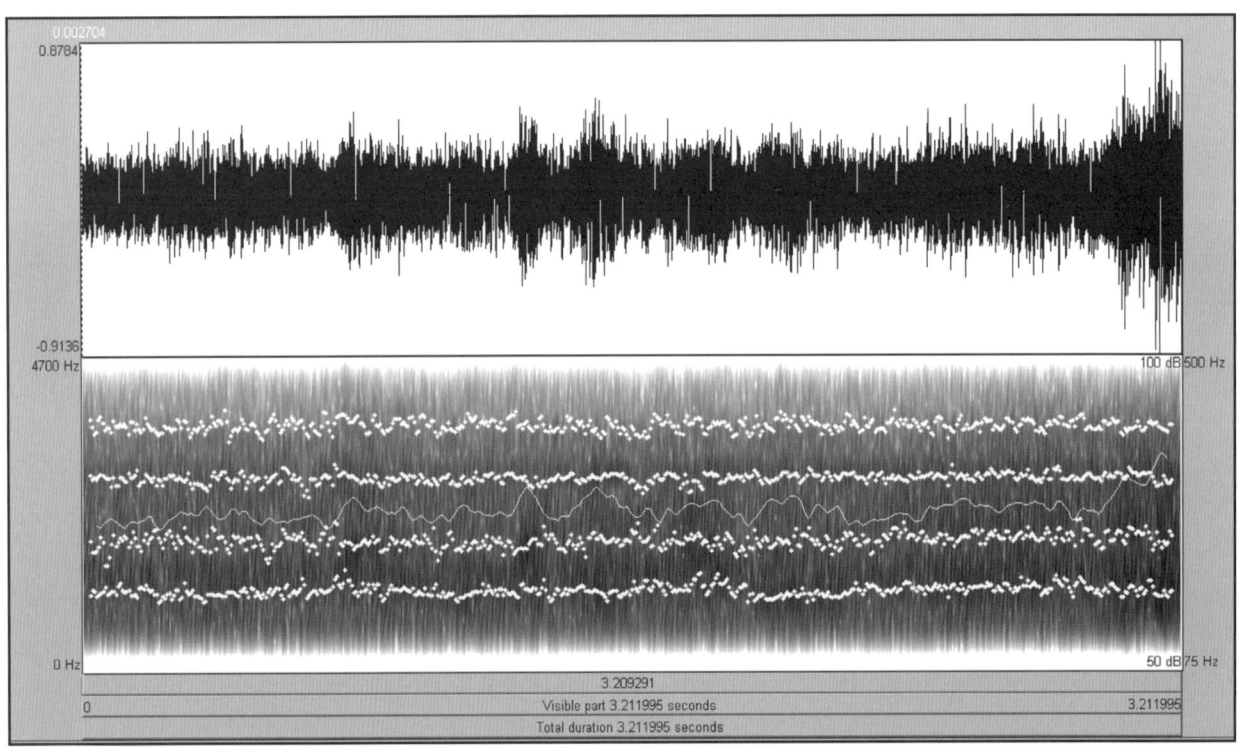

TRACK 74: You can see the solid horizontal line, that denotes audio intensity, combines with the same characteristics as the spectral analysis shows, as a dark background, as the EVP speaks. What is interesting with this file is that there are no pulses or pitch associated with the recording, so it would be difficult to prove that this is a human voice. This one is left up to interpretation.

> "You f***in' tell someone who cares! F***ing bitch!"

It's bad enough that spirits speak in this way which only goes to show that people are people even when they are dead. So I will not add the audio clips from these kinds of spirits.

That's not to say that there are demons racing all around the inn! Nothing could be further from the truth. Spirits will mess with you as you record because they know you will hear them. Sometimes they are angry and will let you know. All the bad voices were recorded in the basement, as is the case in a lot of houses I have recorded in. One theory is that the bad energy is one of heaviness and sinks to the lowest portion of the location. It's an accumulation of the bad things that happen within every house, and the energy needs to go somewhere. It sinks into the basement and lingers. There, the people of like vibratory states of being, can use this bad energy for their own use. This has been told to me from several reputable mediums I have dealt with over many investigations.

There are many more voices that have made themselves known in that one single night, more than most of the investigations I have recorded on. In just over two hours of recording time 70 clips were collected! That's an amazing amount of data from one single evening with such a short duration of recorded time.

If you wish to contact Robyne Marie, you may do so at 781-866-3435. She is a spirit counselor, medium and paranormal investigator. Her talents are far and wide and she is one of the nicest people you will find in the field of paranormal research. She can also be reached by email at luv2bewitchu@aol.com and also www.lightsoutradioshow.com.

You may reach Paul Stream and Bob Marcey at the Inn at Washington Square at 978-741-4997. They are open to paranormal groups who wish to spend a night or two collecting data from this Victorian cache of spirit activity. Please book well in advance to secure your stay.

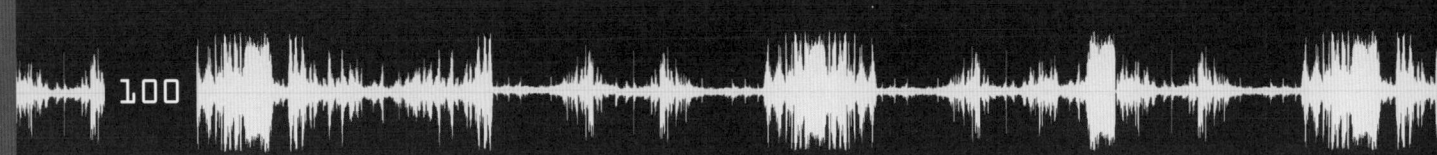

15

The Fearing Tavern Wareham

Circa 1690

**11 Elm Street
Wareham, MA 02571**

The Fearing Tavern was destined to become a paranormal hotspot as an investigation on November 15, 2008 and revealed some startling evidence in the form of EVPs. The Wareham Historical Society, who owns the building, wanted to open the tavern up to the paranormal community so they might gather data during their stay.

The tavern has a wonderful feel to it as it doesn't look as though it has changed at all in all the years it has been standing. The fireplaces look as inviting as the bar does and you can almost see the Revolutionary War heroes sitting at the tables drinking ale and grog. It was at this place that the stage coach would stop and let the travelers out for refreshments for many years.

The one thing that I noticed about the preservation was the thresholds found in every doorway on the interior. They are well worn down after hundreds of years of feet have made them smooth. One can almost imagine the footwear they must have born traveling over them. Just as smooth are the wide pine floors and the banister at the front entrance worn by years of hands looking for help with the climb. The period furniture and artifacts adorn this time capsule of a tavern and you just have to marvel at the great job the Historical Society did bringing the Tavern back to its original glory!

With such an old building spanning three centuries, it sure has seen its fair share of history. It is one of Wareham's earliest homes and it became the Fearing

The haunted Fearing Tavern, Wareham, Massachusetts.

Tavern around 1747 with additions added in 1765 and 1820. It remained with the Fearing family for 200 years with its sixteen period rooms containing authentic eighteenth and nineteenth century furnishings, toys, tools, and many decorative and useful objects.

The Fearing Tavern is believed to be Wareham's oldest house and during the War of 1812, more than 200 British marines marched to the tavern before burning a cotton factory. They must have had their fill of food and ale before setting off on their mission. Inside the house, you'll get an idea of what tavern life was like during the Revolutionary days, minus the wine, ale, and grog. The tavern served at various times as the town's court house and post office. Some residents will tell you that more souls were saved and more town business was conducted over "victuals and grog" than in the meeting-house pews. A good many of the gatherings at Benjamin Fearings Tavern were disgruntled ruminations on the offenses of the British crown.

A 1999 *Standard-Times* article wrote:

> "The tavern is one of five properties throughout the town maintained by the historical society. Restored in 1958, the 16-room, two-story structure is made up of three sections. The oldest

The Fearing Tavern

The beautiful colonial bar.

dates from 1690, and the newest from 1820, but the major section of the white clapboard Georgian Colonial was built in 1765 by tavern-keeper Benjamin Fearing. "In this house, we go back and forth over 300 years," said Ms. Wright. The Fearings were one of the founding families of Wareham, and the marvelously restored rooms in the museum reflect their lives. The front parlors hold family Bibles, portraits of family members and actual Fearing furniture donated by descendants. With such personal items, it's easy to take a trip through time.

The Fearing Tavern was brought to my attention by Tim Weisberg, host of *Spooky South Coast* radio. He was looking for someone to take the lead on EVP recording as part of a team he was putting together for an investigation of the 300-year-old tavern at the request of the owners. The owners wanted to see if any real evidence could be revealed, since it had such a reputation for being haunted.

The team consisted of Tim Weisberg, who brought along his Shack Box which is a version of a Franks' Box. (This device is covered in chapter one.) Also on board was Matt Moniz, the science advisor to the radio program, Andy Lake, who is a paranormal researcher and would set up his video equipment to capture any physical activity that might arise. Carl Wood was an avid fan of all things paranormal and provided the photography. There were also other people who were there as friends and workers of the Wareham Historical Society for a total of about twelve people. That's a bit much for an investigation but everyone came together as a team and got the job done.

Carolyn McMorrow was there on behalf of the historical society and to oversee the investigation to make sure all the artifacts stayed in tact, which they did. Carolyn has a great understanding of the history of the house and its belongings. She herself also cooks over a roaring fire in a cast iron caldron. It has been reported that these meals are outstanding and will satisfy even the hungriest of patriots!

The evening wore on as the investigators moved from room to room, the floors creaking as they went. Question after question was asked in hopes that someone would answer them.

Tim Weisberg asked this question:

"Do you live in this house?"

The response was a surprising:

"Ze attic."

[Play track 75]

One of the many fireplaces.

This is a very clear EVP, but it is low in volume. There is also something that sounds like a broom being applied to the floor, then a sweep is heard. Surprisingly, this recording was made with my Sony handheld recorder and it gives great results, as is apparent here. There is even a bit of reverb with the voice that almost matches the attic space. "Ze attic" sounds like maybe he is of German descent or maybe somewhere close to that area. What a great piece of evidence.

This next file is striking! I have absolutely no explanation as to how or why it was recorded. The sound was not heard by anyone in the tavern at the time and the object producing the sound is an allusive one. I will let you play the file first, so you may be surprised by the sound.

> This clip demonstrates that EVPs are not constrained to just voices. In the beginning, you will hear the investigators talking amongst themselves and then something else happens. It is clear that there is no such object that can make this sound found in the tavern.

The sound resembles an iron door or gate slamming shut and then latching with a large amount of reverb! Right afterwards, there is a man's voice that says,

> "Christ did penance."

[Play Track 76]

Wow, was I surprised when this played through my headphones! I wasn't expecting anything like this as I'd never recorded anything like it before. What was the point of the door slamming shut? This EVP is truly an amazing find! I just don't know what to make of it as I play it over and over.

And if that weren't enough, have a listen to the little girl who asks,

> "Wanna play dress up?"

just as I was heading down to the basement.

[Play track 77]

Her voice is a bit in the background, but is clearly audible. I wonder who she is as her name was not revealed to us in any of the recordings made that night. In fact, this is the only child EVP captured.

This clip was recorded in the control area in the central part of the house. A voice of a man very clearly states,

> "We got 'em mouse holes in here."

[Play track 78]

His voice has an accent to it and is so clear you'd think it was one of the

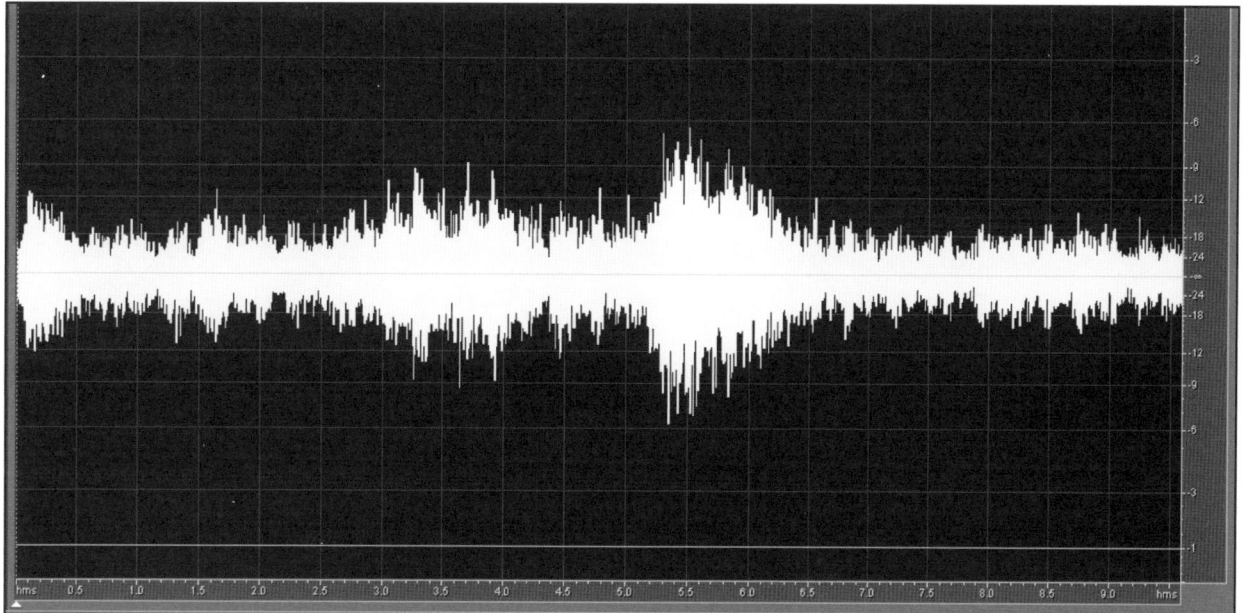

TRACK 76: This is a screen shot of Cool Edit's decibel characteristic. You can actually see just where on the track the large iron gate slams shut. The wider the vertical pattern is, the louder the sound is in decibels.

investigators! But obviously it isn't, and why would anyone say a thing like that during an investigation? Who would think of that? It kind of sounds like something someone would say from the old west.

The Fearing Tavern kept handing me one awesome EVP after another! This next one has become one of my favorites. When I play it for people and tell them where it was recorded, there is a look of surprise that comes to their face and rightfully so.

There is a spot on the floor in that basement that sounds like it may be hollow underneath. The theory goes that, at one time, it may have been a secret entrance to an underground tunnel that leads to a waterway. It is said that it was used in the Underground Railroad to move people from the nearby waterway into a tunnel that starts at the nail factory just across the street. From there, a small boat could just disappear underneath the building and reappear on the other side without its passengers.

The tunnel was designed to bring water to the nail factory by way of a bucket that could be lowered from the inside of the building. The back side of this tunnel has been sealed up and it is doubtful if any real documentation can be found linking it to the Underground Railroad but the hollow sounding floor is very intriguing.

One of the investigators brushes off the cement floor with his foot, and

The Fearing Tavern

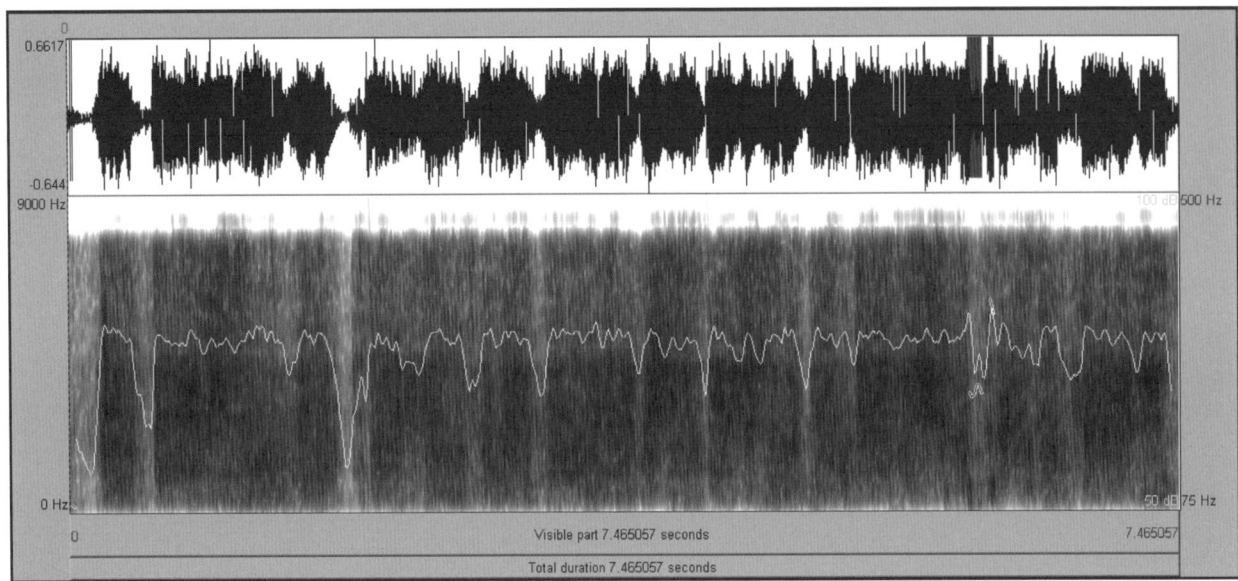

TRACK 79: What an amazing screenshot this is, as it clearly shows the EVP riding the crest of the strength of the sound wave. This is from the first half of the file in which the EVP says, "Hey Ashford, I killed Grandpa Ash! I just knew that you'd feel the pain." In the bottom portion, there is shown a squiggly horizontal line which is in regard to "intensity." The darkened background also shows the same characteristic. I believe that the EVP is using the strong audio frequency of a foot sweeping dirt from the floor to communicate with.

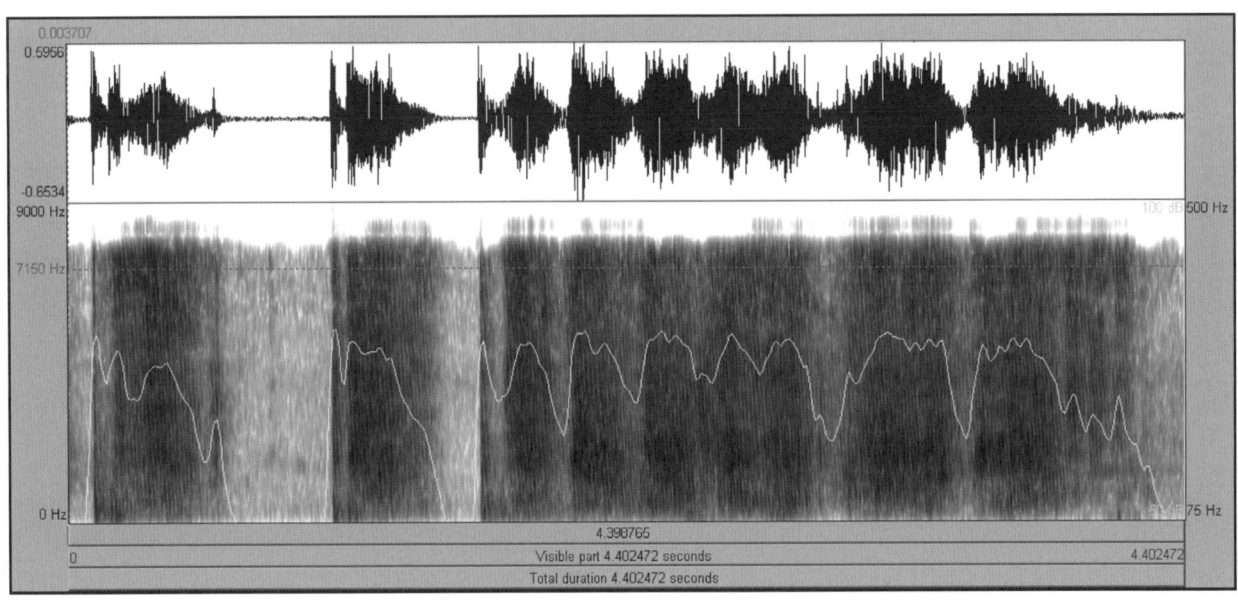

TRACK 79.5: The second half of the file, the EVP states, "Then con...sider it a...a gift." This screenshot shows even more clearly the strength in intensity and in overall decibels this EVP is surfing on.

over that sound, you can hear a voice. This voice is admitting to murder! The grandfather is the victim here and if we go by what is being told to us, then it must have been one of the grandchildren who did the killing. Apparently, there were at least two grandchildren; one could not kill and the other one could! The one who can is the one speaking and confesses as if he is having a conversation with the other one—like it was recent.

The voice says,

"Hey Ashford,
I killed Grandpa Ash!
I just knew that
you'd feel the pain!"

The person who is sweeping the floor with his foot stops for a few seconds and then continues and so does the voice.

"Then con…sider it a…
a gift!"

[Play track 79]

This is one of the most surprising EVP recordings I have to date! Never have I captured anything like it! Its strength has a command over the sound of the floor being swept and is not a very pleasant sounding voice at all. The voice is also in perfect time with the investigator's foot sweeping the floor. How do they know exactly when this will happen? Twice! He almost sounds happy that he killed Grandpa! Even if Grandpa wasn't a very good person, why would someone kill him? There is much more to this picture than we know and research must be done to verify the name *Ashford,* and if there is a match, then the obituaries may be the next step.

However, if the murder was from a very long time ago, then there may never be an answer to any of the questions surrounding this little story. After all, it may have looked like an accident so it would not draw too much attention.

There was a piece of video footage that was captured too and is very interesting. The footage shows a single bright light anomaly travel through the air blinking before disappearing into the wall. This light was nicknamed *Tinkerbelle* after its characteristics.

The Fearing Tavern has yielded some of the finest EVPs from one evening's recording sessions that I have ever done. There were more than fifty EVPs that I picked up, and there needs to be more investigating of this tremendous resource of audio phenomena to determine if it is truly haunted. However, based on the evidence, I can't see how it couldn't be!

16

First Parish Church Norwell

24 River Street
P. O. Box 152
Norwell, MA 02061

This investigation came to fruition over friendly conversation one Friday night between my wife, Paula, and Victoria Weinstein, the minister of the First Church. Victoria—Vicky—asked how my ghost hunting was going and was promptly updated. She mentioned that her church experienced frequent spiritual activity and would I be interested in recording there? One text message later and I had a church to record in. You have to love technology! I spoke to Vicky on Saturday to get the low down and was off on another adventure in the world of the paranormal from a church.

This was no ordinary church. Although it was built in 1830, the congregation dates all the way back to 1642! The records that are contained there have all the activity that was recorded since that time and there are also many photographs of the past ministers near the front entrance. There are artifacts in a glass case, as well as letters and documents. It is clear that history is important to this congregation, and rightfully so, since it was the Pilgrims who founded it just twenty years after landing in Plymouth!

I have always felt that history was an important factor when investigating any old house or building. It gives you a special insight on the events from years gone by. But this church doesn't have any murders or ran sackings that have been reported, so why would it have paranormal activity going on?

The following was taken from the church's web site and contains information of the beginnings of it's parish:

A haunted church?

Originally Scituate included what are now the towns of Hanover, Norwell, and Scituate. Hanover became a separate town in 1727, our section became South Scituate in 1849 and the name was changed to Norwell in 1888. The First Parish of Scituate was established in 1634 and the meeting house was erected on Meeting House Lane just below the old cemetery as you go toward the ocean. The spot is not marked but there is a hollow place on the right hand side which is where most believe the meeting house stood; also a tablet in the graveyard refers to it. The Scituate church was not a united one from the first. Mr. Giles Saxton served as minister for a short time followed by Mr. John Lothrop, who a few years later because of disagreement in regard to baptism, moved with quite a number of the congregation to Barnstable. This is the same issue Mr. Lothrop experienced in his church in England. Mr. Lothrop belonged to the liberal party, and wearying of the controversy, took a major portion of the congregation to Barnstable. In 1641, Mr. Charles Chauncy, a man of most distinguished talents became the next pastor. Possessed of an ardent temper, and impatient of opposition, he thought that his own talents should be enough in themselves to overcome any opposition to his views. He soon found himself in trouble with the authorities in England, and finding no security there, he fled to the new world, reaching Plymouth in 1637. The Rev. Charles Chauncy was a scholar and theologian, also skilled in law and medicine who held many strong opinions, the most controversial of which was the form of baptism. The gist of the controversy, as noted in Bradford's History, was that Mr. Chauncy held that baptism "ought only to be by dipping, and putting ye whole body under water, and that sprinkling was unlawful." The dissidents, who were the liberal faction, wanted freedom of choice in the mode of baptism and preferred the simpler method of "sprinkling." They admitted that "immersion or dipping was lawful, but in this coulde countrie be not so conveniente." Mr. Chauncy, who was a progressive and intelligent churchman in so many ways, was stubborn and unyielding when it came to the question of baptism. It was his way or no way. The end result was that the sprinklers moved up river to form a more liberal church.

It is amazing to be able to read this kind of detail about the goings on from this church from so long ago. You can get a perspective that can be found no where else.

William Witherell

(1645-1684)

As a result of this controversy, the Second Church was established February 2, 1642, by those with the more liberal ideas. William Vassall was the leader of the liberals and in all probability the first meetings were held in his home at Belle House Neck which stood near the present junction of Neal Gate Street and Route 3A overlooking the North River.

The first minister was William Witherell, and the meeting house was located on Wilson Hill, Main Street, at the corner of Old Meeting House Lane. It was a small frame building with thatch roof and no glass in the windows, just oiled paper. This was used by the society for the thirty-nine years Mr. Witherell served as pastor. He lived nearby but the house he occupied was not owned by the Society. There is a boulder marking the supposed site of the meeting house. Originally there was a small cemetery but later this land was used for farming purposes and the then owner removed the old grave stones and is said to have destroyed them completely.

Mr. Witherell's record of baptisms begins in September, 1645, with that of one of his own children, "Anno 1645 Sarah, ye daughter of Wm. Wetherell, Septbre 7." This record, numbering 608 baptisms, appears in his own handwriting until 1674, when a paralytic affliction compelled him to employ assistance in such work. This large number of baptisms during the thirty-nine years of Mr. Witherell's ministry, large indeed for a country church in a sparsely settled district, in those early days, is evidence in itself that ministers of Mr. Witherell's popularity because of the broadness of his views regarding church membership, as well as that of infant sprinkling, was an uncommon one. Parents brought their children to him for baptism from as far away as Yarmouth on the Cape.

Mr. Chauncy left Scituate in 1654 and became president of Harvard University while Mr. Dunster left the presidency of Harvard to become pastor of the First Church of Scituate. Mr. Dunster died in 1659, and his successor was Nicholas Baker of Hingham. He and Mr. Witherell were both kindly tolerant men, so together they managed to end the long feud between the First and Second Churches. Today both the First Parish in Scituate and the First Parish in Norwell are liberal Unitarian churches and members of the Unitarian Universalist Association.

This is just a small fraction of the history that can be found about this wonderful church and what a tremendous effort it must have been to continue with the archiving of such detail for hundreds of years! The church still archives all of its business as well as its sermons. There is even a documented time capsule that was locked up on December 20, 1992 under the direction of R.M. Fewkes. It is to be opened in the year 2042 which will be the 400th anniversary of the parish! That's a long time in United States years! What a coincidence that he writes "We hope and pray that some of those who are alive and with us this day, our children, will be present with you on December 21, 2042 and can provide a living link between our generation and yours. Most of us will be dead and buried, but we will be with you in spirit." Spirit indeed!

When I entered the old church by the side entrance the inside looked quite new but that changes when you walk into the sanctuary. That is where the history lies within the pulpit, pews and balcony. The pews still have the little doors on them that must be opened to gain entrance for seating. It was very popular back in those days to have your own family pew. If you donated well and regularly then you may in effect rent your own seat in the church. You could even paint it your own colors I am told.

After some conversation with Vicky, the current minister, and Carrie, a member of the congregation, I set up my microphones in the corners of the sanctuary and one on the pulpit. I also had my handheld recorder. Victoria said her blessings and left the building, she was preparing for her first sabbatical. I am glad Carrie stayed with me because the following hours spent in this old church would be one of the most memorable investigations I have had to date! I started asking the usual questions like, "Is there anyone here that would like to speak to us?"

Almost instantly, activity started in the balcony. There is an original pipe organ that was installed at the time the church was built. It is being repaired and the pipes were spread out on the floor of the balcony. Carrie and I could hear footsteps of someone walking around up there. All of the activity seemed to be coming from the right hand side. This was unusual because it was loud and persistent.

This track has been amplified so it is more easily heard and lasts 43 seconds.

[Play track 80]

This is just how we were hearing this activity! Truly amazing! I ask if Carrie heard those people because I just had a hard time believing what I was hearing.

The church still has the original bell in its tower as well and rings on the hour. This next clip has the bell ringing and a female voice that says,

"Get out."

Then a male voice low in volume says,

"Yeh!"

[Play track 81]

This clip is in its original recorded volume because of the bell ringing. We were still hearing footsteps, and voices were now appearing up in that balcony.

Carrie felt that maybe it was the bell ringer who was up there, so I asked if they were responsible for ringing the bell on time?

There is a male EVP that says my name as I start the sentence.

[Play track 82]

The recording equipment hard at work.

One haunted balcony!

I was hearing the voice of a man becoming prominent and Carrie could hear it too which made me a bit nervous. Although I have heard thousands of EVP come across my headphones, it is altogether different when you hear it live, right in front of you! But I wasn't scared, just apprehensive, and maybe a little nervous. I had no fear at anytime during this investigation.

The man's voice came through loud as he says the name

"Quinn."

And right after there is a women's voice that says,

"Mrs. Quinn."

[Play track 83]

This was heard by the both of us! You can hear my excitement in this clip! Who is Quinn? Was that really the man's wife? It's almost like she understood the way her husband's voice would sound and spoke up to get the name across to me. I have never heard so much activity and voices that appear so often when I'd asked questions before! This church was proving to be a hot spot for paranormal activity, especially from the balcony. Usually I hear the voices after they have been recorded, but I was hearing them as they were being spoken! And Carrie was hearing them too, so she proved to be a valuable asset in this evening's investigation because no one would have believed my story otherwise.

In this next clip, I had asked,

"Who was in the balcony? Can you tell us your name?"

There are two names that were recorded.

"Sandwich"

and

"Quinn."

[Play track 84]

The name *Sandwich* is very clear and *Quinn* remains the same in volume and a bit lower in clarity. Ten decibels in volume have been added to help with hearing of the voices. That is the only alteration that has been made in any of these recordings.

This next track is another recording of the male EVP saying Quinn again except he said it next to me! He had moved from the balcony down to the middle of the room where I was standing! And both Carrie and I heard it loud and clear!

[Play track 85]

The pulpit at Christmas time.

First Parrsih Church

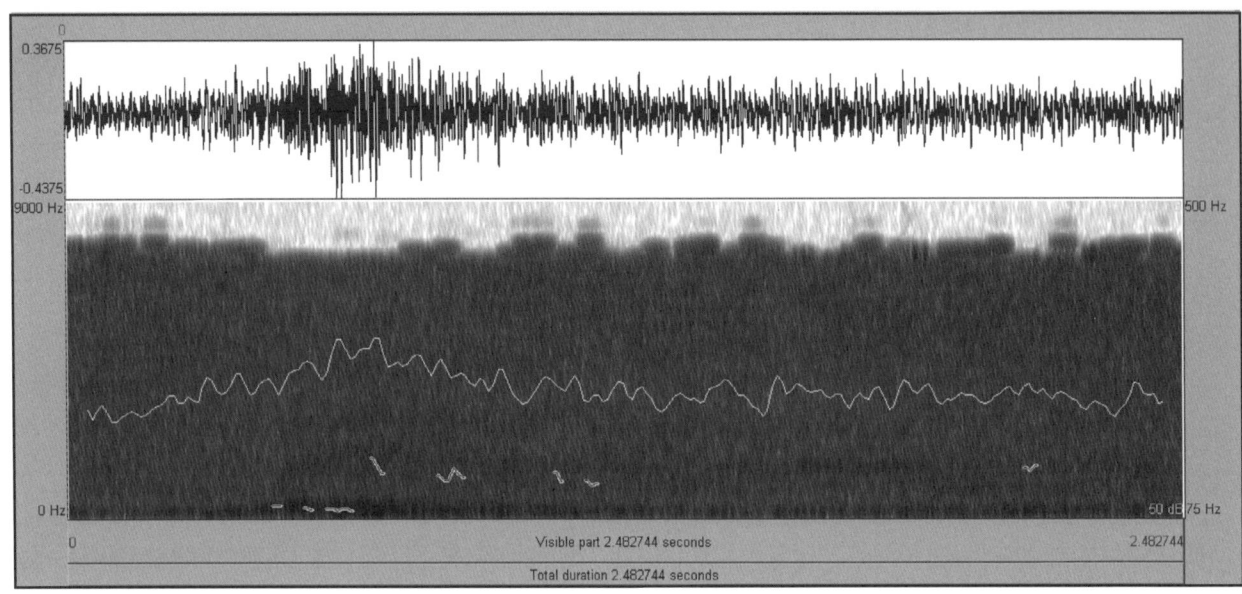

TRACK 85: You can see the rise in intensity as the male EVP speaks the name "Quinn."

After the name Quinn is spoken, you will hear my camera take a picture, then Carrie and I talk about the voice we both just heard! This man, Quinn, was very eager to have his name known. Three times I have heard him speaking it, and his wife said it, too. Who is Quinn? This is a name, along with Sandwich, that needs further research to find out if he has an affiliation with this church.

Meanwhile, the footsteps and clanging around continued as the night wore on. This next clip shows the heightened activity from the balcony.

You can hear the footsteps more clearly.

[Play track 86]

Carrie and I just kept looking at each other in disbelief at how loud the activity was. I just have never experienced anything like it before. It sounded like there were movers up in the balcony, moving furniture around. I have to remind the reader that there was a padlock on the door to the balcony to keep anyone from going up there and disturbing the tubes of the pipe organ as they lay on the floor awaiting reassembly.

The voice belonging to Quinn came through again, but this time he says,

"Women."

I believe he says a sentence but it is not clear enough to make out.

[Play track 87]

The track has ten decibels added to it so the reader can hear it more clearly. Most of the recordings taken that night were low in volume but needed nothing other than a little bit of amplification to be heard.

With all the history of this parish, it is no doubt spirits are eager to speak to us. The other parishioners have reported that they have seen and heard many spirits in the sanctuary, but feel that they are friendly in nature. I believe this to be true as well, since fear was not present during this investigation for myself or Carrie.

There is a comfortable sense of being when walking around the sanctuary as the voices ooze from its framework. Boots and shoes walk about the wooden floors, still busy after all these years. Movement in the balcony is constant at times and I wonder if it might be the choir of days long past shuffling into position.

Why should all this activity be comforting? Why is there no fear? Maybe it's because they are good decent people waiting to hear a good sermon one more time?

If you want to speak to someone at the church you may reach them via email at their web site at:

office@firstparishnorwell.org

The folks there are friendly and helpful and will provide answers to you questions.

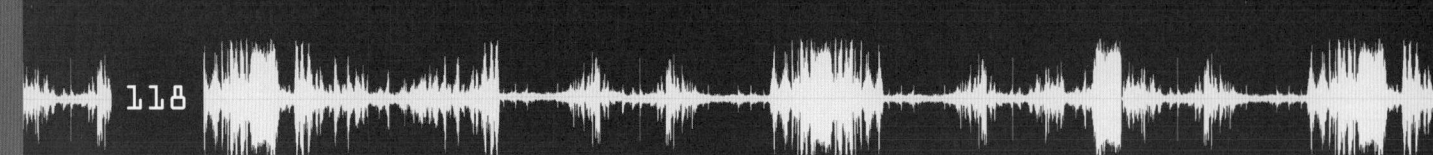

17

The Great Singularity and the Oneness

I have two recordings in a sing-song fashion of a different kind. One of them is unclear as to what is being said and the other one has "hallelujah" being sung. These two recordings have a lot in common and yet they are very uncommon. Common, in that they both are being sung by choirs of people and not by one person in particular. They have mostly sopranos; if there are baritones and basses, I can't hear them very well, but that may be the result of the recorder's parameters. In one, the word "hallelujah" can be heard and I can almost make out that it may be coming from a single person, however, that may be a stretch. You can hear a group of sopranos holding a note that drops and then returns to the same note again. The recording is only a couple of seconds long in duration, however, the message of different dynamics comes across.

[Play Track 88]

Both of these recordings have a choir-like quality associated with them and are very uncommon, in that they represent only two of the thousands of recordings that I have accumulated over the years. These are very special indeed. So what are they?

Where they were recorded is not as relevant, I believe, as the message and the recording itself. I believe I have captured the first *Gates of Heaven* in an audio recording, if that's possible at all. A choir. Why did that get recorded and not a single person speaking or even two people having a conversation, as with all the rest of my recordings numbering in the thousands?

After thinking about it for quite some time, I came to the conclusion, based on their point of view, their world of existence. If we are to assume that we will be free from our bodies and living as spirit, then our communication with others must come from within ourselves without the use of a voice box. This

The Great Singularity and the Oneness

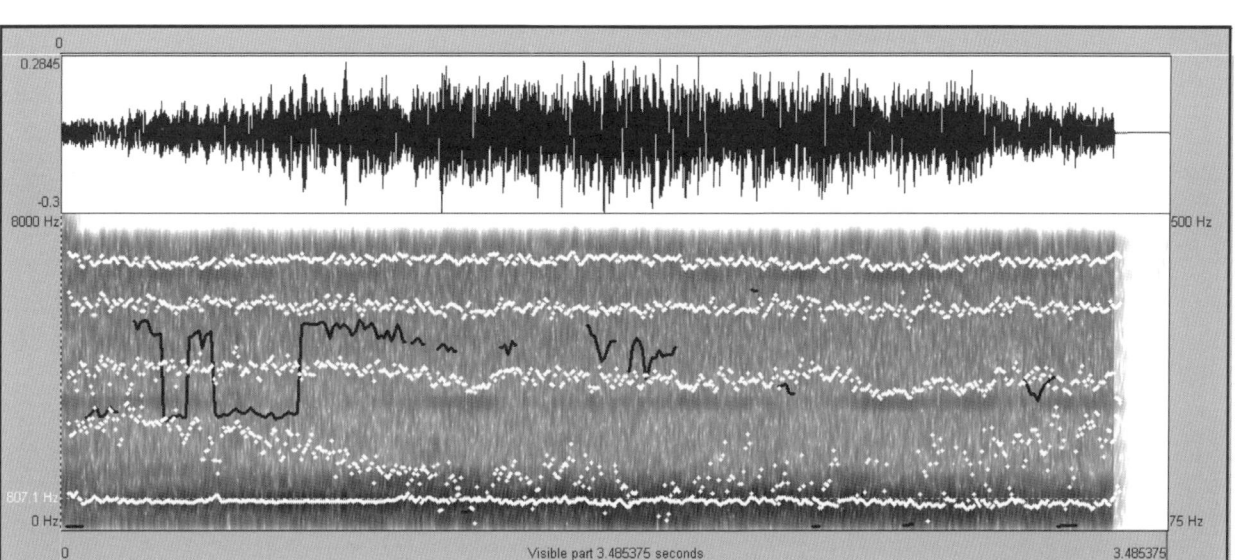

TRACK 88: There is no question that this track contains human voices as the screenshot from PRATT clearly shows. It has all of the information to properly identify it as human speaking voices. The bottom half of the screen shot clearly shows tight formant formation and a great deal of pitch. The upper portion of the screen shot shows strong pulses necessary for identification of the human voice.

is done using your mind, as you think others will hear it. Now, when you have risen from the Great Singularity and enter the first stage of Heaven, you will have learned to shed that kind of life as singular and will accept and be accepted in the lives of others as one life, meaning you will now be sharing the lives of everyone around you and they will share in yours. All that you are and have been will be seen and felt just as you lived it by everyone else.

What will you gain with that? Knowledge, in a sense, that can only be gained by such a process. Extra consciousness, if you will, which can only be magnified and obtained in a non-physical body. In that place, choirs of people are singing out in praise with their minds and souls for something that is worthy of it. One can only imagine they are singing in praise of God. Why? Because they are closer to Him than the people who belong in the Great Singularity and want nothing more than to be part of the inner circle of worship of the Devine Creator. It is, after all, the very first step into the hall of holies as people become one in open mind and spirit of resonant song, where everything that makes you who you are is shared with everyone else who is in the same place as you. Resonant song is lifted up from within you as you gain the prize of consciousness from everyone else around you completely, being aware

The Great Singularity and the Oneness

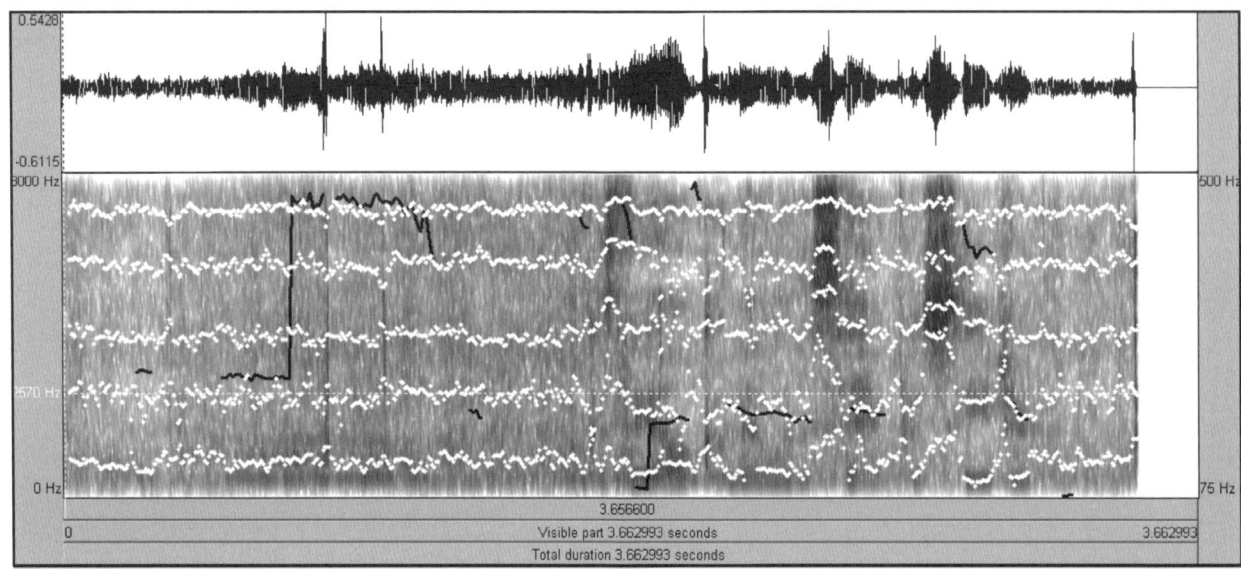

TRACK 89: Here again we see the same human characteristics from this file as the previous one. There are strong pitch and pulse characteristics and even somewhat strong formants. Half way through, an investigator says, "cause they all come through with their own procedure." You can see a real human speaking on the screen print and the three dark areas to the right keynote decibel strength from her voice. An odd note is that when looking at this file with PRATT, one can notice that there is more pitch in the choir singing, as an EVP, than the actual person speaking. This must be to due the signal strength the recorder had at the time of the recording, in other words a person may have been off to my right when the recording was made.

the whole time of the close proximity of God.

The recording reveals "Hallelujah" being sung by many and you can barely make out a singular person.

As I recorded on the edge of the Hockomock Swamp in East Bridgewater on the Old Stage Coach Road with my Sony handheld digital recorder, a unique message came through. Someone wanted me to hear that, so as they sang, everyone else came through as well because they are one. This place I call the Oneness for lack of a better term. It is the first true step into experiencing the reality of who God really is. To know Him is to graduate through life in steps for experience and to gain the knowledge of unrealized preparedness. You can't move on unless you graduate life itself just like you can't be accepted into Harvard without any form of previous education.

When you listen to the clip, keep in mind it was recorded with a handheld digital recorder. Trying to get a high fidelity recording with that is like trying to win NASCAR race with a horse-drawn buggy. I like to use the following analogy

The Great Singularity and the Oneness

when trying to describe the presence the recording provides. Imagine that you are standing right next to Niagara Falls. You have with you a handheld digital recorder that you use to record the mighty sound that tons of water makes as it plummets over the cliff face. You bring it back home to play for your family and friends but when you press play, all you get is a loud rumbling sound. This is due mostly to the digital recorder's capabilities. It has one or two microphones for stereo recording, and the frequencies of what it records, on both ends of the spectrum, have been cut for "clarity." The low sounds only go so low and the high sounds only go so high. This recording really cannot convey the whole experience that visiting Niagara Falls has to offer. All you have left is rumbling in place of the smell and spray of the water, the rocks that have been shaken and loosened by years of erosion, the wind, or the crowds of people that stand in the presence of such a mighty natural wonder, sharing their joy at what they are experiencing.

The recording of the Oneness cannot convey the experience of being there or what it has to offer. You have to listen to what the recording reveals, which is "no body" singing in a swamp.

[Play tracks 88 and 89]

Pareidolia: Random or vague sound that is perceived as significant. Your brain will make sense of something that is possibly senseless.

Use both external speakers and headphones when reviewing your audio files. Pareidolia can creep in after long hours of listening.

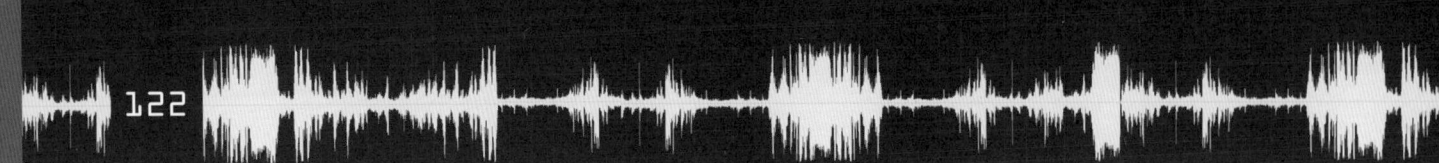

18

Becoming Clairaudient

It was never my intention to actually gain some sort of psychic or otherwise paranormal ability to hear EVPs. However, after recording many sessions at a local historical site called Sachem Rock and collecting many EVPs from that site, I got to know a voice known as Bethany. As I collected the data, a story unfolded as to who this person was. However, I kept running into dead ends. Every time I did the research to find out who this person was, I was unable to verify the data given to me. It seemed I was being led in circles.

I continued, though, because this voice and the others were fascinating to me. One of the only death threats that I have recorded came from this place, and when I asked who this person was, the response was Satan. It was kind of spooky at first to know that you had been possibly communicating with a demon but there are a lot of people on that side that are going to tell you things that simply are not true. And I believe this was the case here. I found later in the following years that you cannot always count on actual answers to your questions.

After a short recording session at the historical site, I went home and went about the day. Later on that evening, I transferred the files from my handheld recorder to my laptop computer. When I got to the end of that particular session, I was in my car and about to leave. It said,

"I will see you later; hope all is well."

and then drove away. However, when analyzing that particular clip I found the voice to say,

"I will see you tonight in your room."

Well, it was tonight and I was in my room. So is this what Bethany meant by she will see me? I got quite a cold chill that ran down my arms and electricity that shot up my spine! What have I done? Have I really invited a spirit into my home? How do I get rid of it? This is where the danger can lie in doing paranormal research without having any means of getting rid of something you do not want.

But in my case it was too late. She was here! What have I done!? Will my family be involved or affected by this unwanted entity? These thoughts were racing through my mind and panic set in. All I wanted to do was to stop the session and just ignore it and maybe it would all go way. So I started another question and answering session while using my computer; by this I mean I would ask a question with my recorder on and then I would transfer the file into my computer to listen to the voice. This went on for several hours as the voice did not come back in a steady fashion, but came and went as time went on.

But it was late, around one o'clock in the morning, and I was getting very tired. I had been recording for all hours and the room seemed to be filled with electricity as I tried to rid this spirit from my presence. The voice started to tell me things that I did not want to hear and it told me to do things that I did not want to do. This was very scary, as I thought I was in the presence of a succubus, a female evil spirit that preys on men during their sleep. I did not want this to happen to me so I started to pray because that is all that I knew to do at that point as the fear set in strong. This is the kind of fear that is felt when you are in big trouble, really big trouble.

At this time, I recorded another voice telling Bethany that she is not welcome here and she is to leave and never return. This new voice called itself Pat and she would watch over me. This was music to my soul. The ride was over, but it seemed I had opened up a window that I could not close. Now I had Pat to deal with, but at least she was seemingly helpful. I was still very unsettled.

I took the headphones off and shut down the computer hoping that my prayers would be answered and the Spirit would leave. I was wrong! I could hear the same voice speaking to me in the same fashion as the whispering in EVPs that I had been recording! But my equipment was shut down, how could this be?

There was also an electrical popping sound coming from a specific location in the room which I understood sometimes happens with the paranormal. Now it was happening to me! The room was silent and full of electricity, me, and whoever Bethany was. So I started to pray again asking for the help from anyone who would listen, including Jesus.

I found strength during my prayer session and I allowed the fear to leave my mind. I believe this was the turning point of getting rid of something that I did not want, paranormally speaking. I had removed the fuel for the Spirit to feed on nearby, taking the wind out of its sails. Maybe this kept the spirit from becoming a full-bodied apparition right before my eyes? I was so tired at this point, that I shut the light off and went to sleep.

Here, I want to mention that since the birth of my daughter, we have had the baby monitor on so that we can hear the sound-making device play a sound of running water to aid in our daughter's sleep and ours.

On the first night following that particular session, or should I say run in, I turned the baby monitor on to prepare for bed. Upon closing my eyes to drift off to sleep, I noticed a voice speaking to me over the sound of flowing water that was coming through the speaker. My eyes bolted open, and I said to myself, *She is still here!*

The previous night had been stressful and exhausting. I'd just wanted to go to sleep, but I'd needed to deal with Bethany now that she was speaking to me. I was still very unsettled but Bethany was gone, for now.

I said my prayers and I fell asleep hoping that this would take care of myself and my family. I woke the next day feeling refreshed and just a bit nervous about the voice. After all, it was just a voice and I believed that. So now what can I do as it continues every night?

One of the amazing discoveries that I have made is that when it is very quiet I can hear the same voice in my ear as an EVP. This is known as being clairaudient, but I had never known of this particular ability that some people possessed until some time later. Several spirit voices have come and gone during the year since it all started. There has been Pat, the Teacher, and even my deceased mother.

I know what the reader must be thinking, he's schizophrenic, right? But since I am aware of these audible voices; it can't be schizophrenia. They appear just like the EVPs I have been recording.

These voices have led me on many adventures, somewhat. I had asked this voice for the winning number in the lottery and it delivered. It gave me the winning numbers of the Mega Millions lottery game that paid out about $100 million. How lucrative could this field be? If this number came in, I would have quite a story to tell. However, later that evening, a different voice, my mom, told me to rip up the ticket. I said are you crazy? This is a $100 million ticket! Why would I rip it up? The voice told me because I am receiving information from an unknown spiritual source and I am doing their bidding. Reluctantly, I actually ripped up the winning lottery ticket! This was a test of faith on my part and I understood what I had to do. The next day when the number came out, I noticed mine was not even close. So the lesson was learned.

Another adventure was when a meeting was to take place between myself and a member of the Illuminati. A voice told me that he was located in California and he knew who I was. He has been monitoring my conversations via the voices. This was very strange and I couldn't understand what this had to do with anything. He told me that this ability was rare in the form that I had and he would set up a meeting that would explain everything.

A date and time was set up for me to meet someone arriving in a black limousine right out front of my place of work. Now I was very skeptic. I had read of the Illuminati in a book a long time ago but this is ridiculous! If there really was anything to my ability, this would prove it beyond a shadow of a doubt! I went out to the front of my work place at the date and time that was given, sat down on the bench, and waited. No one came. No limo, no nothing. I revisited the unnamed voice and he told me that the driver was at the wrong location, so a second meeting was set up. Again I went outside and sat on the bench to wait for the limo. What a surprise, nothing happened. I was relieved and disappointed at the same time. The answer that I got for the cancelled meeting was that I had done something to negate the meeting. Then the voice was gone, never to return.

What a strange and exciting journey I have had with these voices. They were all harmless except Bethany who caused a lot of fear. Other than that, they were all fine and they were just voices.

After about a year of this communicating, I put forth a thought in my mind and I heard it come out of the speaker! Whoa! Wait a minute. I did it again and again. The result was the same. Every time I spoke a thought in my mind, I would hear it as an EVP coming out of the baby monitor, light and airy! The same held true without the monitor in a quiet environment as before but this time it was coming from me. When I stopped speaking the "other" voice would continue. I soon realized that what I was hearing was, besides my own thoughts, my own subconscious. Is this even possible?

Now I felt very safe knowing I had been dealing with myself all of that time. I was in control and had no more fear.

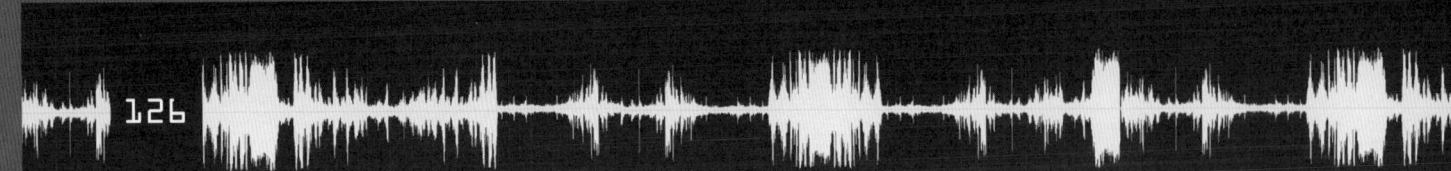

Conclusions

I would like to include some things to look for if and when the reader starts to record for themselves. Yes, the EVPs are human-sounding voices, but there are oddities to be found in the way they will sound when they are recorded. Remember they are well *outside the box* of human thinking and understanding, as their reality has changed dramatically. That being said, please bear in mind that you may not always capture the voices you want, nor may the results be that which you may expect. There are many variables at play and all can be taken into consideration as you try to explain the voices.

Just because you have recorded an EVP, doesn't mean you can wholeheartedly trust what they are saying. This would be foolish, just as if you were to believe everything anyone told you. However, the voices are worthy of study and replaying for friends and family. They can speak very fast and you may miss them if you don't know how they sound, so listen for something like a blurp of sound or an odd sound that doesn't belong.

Often times, an EVP will appear between words in the silence in normal conversation. Whispering is the most common way for EVPs to appear, and listening for these kinds of voices does take some practice, so be patient.

There is a theory that may help to explain how it happens. It's based on the fact that energy is never at a constant state of being, much like time. It is always moving and changing in its own strength and weakness. The veil that separates our two worlds behaves in much the same way. It moves back and forth like an ocean wave arriving on the beach or a curtain caught in a breeze. When it is closest to our dimension, say the window, information can be exchanged from their world into ours. The energy from that place is supposed to be at a higher frequency and lighter, and so does not make itself greatly known to us. They can see our world and themselves easily in the way we see ourselves only. Imagine, if you will, having the ability to see the spirit world that easily?

Whispering may be the easiest way for them to communicate as it takes less energy to do so, just like it is here on Earth. I speculate that it may have something to do with the strength of their minds as they try to communicate, as opposed to a voice box. Maybe it depends on how much spiritual energy you have? They have to use their psychic power, and if it's weak, then they may come through as whispers. Newly departed people may require practice to get their "voice" louder. If they are a stronger-minded person, then maybe their voice comes through loud and clear, even more human sounding.

There are also faint voices that are spread out over time that may take ten seconds to complete a simple two or three word sentence. There are very fast, very slow, and normal-speed talkers that will make up your recordings. And with that, they can be very faint and difficult to hear. They can be very loud and easy to hear, or very loud, but unintelligible. There will be several voices speaking together or separately as in a normal conversation. When you hear several spirits talking together, it may help to be able to train your ear to listen to just one voice, so you can understand what they are saying, if that's possible. One voice may be high in frequency and whispery and the other low and with a lot of bass.

Headphones are essential, however, don't use them solely to listen to your files. The results may be different when using external speakers and why this is, I don't fully understand. Results may change the next day you listen to them, because your mental direction of focus has been shifted by relaxing. You won't be so intent on listening to precise detail after a good night's sleep.

Reversing a clip of an EVP is very interesting and often has something to do with the forward message. This is not always the case, but often enough, it is. Why complete sentences are formed in reverse is a strange thing, however, it is real. Just as humans speak in reverse, so too do the spirits. This is an interesting field, and if you search the Internet, you will find a lot of information about it.

Radio cross talk is the bleed over from a radio transmitter that saturates your recording device with its signal, making it appear like an EVP. Or so they say.

This is obviously not an EVP and can easily be distinguished.

[Play track 90]

It has been only very recently in man's search for proof of life after death that we are able to provide any evidence of this phenomenon at all. The use of technology that has been designed to record fine detail and light energy sources has given us this evidence. This in itself has stirred the spiritual pot as more people are communicating with spirits and vice versa. Information is exchanging and being recorded as real data at a rate never before seen. Devices are being created continuously to further open the doorway or lift the veil completely to allow a permanent and direct line of communication with the spirit world.

Let the voices make you think.

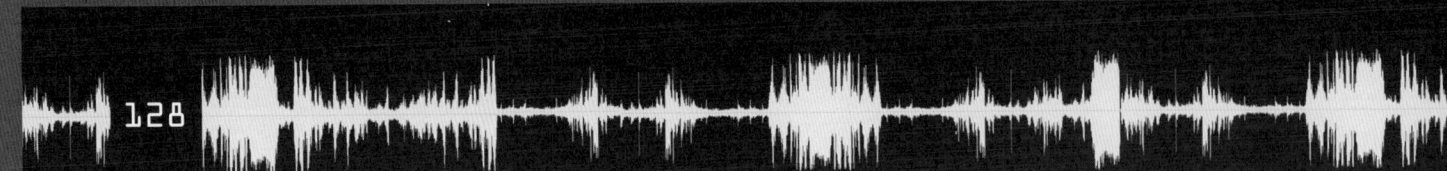

Resources

Wikipedia: EVP, psychoacoustics. wikipedia.org.

Meek, George. "Healers and the Healing." Theosophical Publishing House, 1979.

Meek, George. "After We Die, What Then?" Ariel Press, Oct 1988.

Spooky South Coast radio. Spookysouthcoast.com.

Ghost Chronicles. neghostproject.com.

The Bible, King James Version.

Ghost Hunters. http://www.scifi.com/ghosthunters/ to watch episodes.

East Bridgewater's Most Haunted. http://www.ebctv.org for more information.